THE AUSTRALIAN
Women's Weekly

One of nature's original fast foods, seafood is ideally suited to the way we live today. Clean, fresh, simple, it's easy to prepare, quick to cook, generally low in fat, cholesterol and salt, yet rich in protein, vitamins and minerals... everything we want in our diet in one neat package! But perhaps the best news is that, because of the amazing number of fish and shellfish species that are harvested off our shores, we can enjoy high-quality seafood as often as we like. And *Dinner Seafood* shows us how to make the most of it.

Pamela Clark

Food Director

contents

The quick and easy dinners in this chapter will solve the weeknight dilemma that all busy people face: how to produce a satisfying meal in the shortest possible time that will appeal to everyone in the family.

grilled mahi mahi with roasted corn and chilli salad

PREPARATION TIME 30 MINUTES **COOKING TIME** 25 MINUTES

8 trimmed corn cobs (2kg)
1 egg yolk
1 clove garlic, crushed
2 tablespoons lime juice
1 teaspoon dijon mustard
¾ cup (180ml) olive oil
1 medium red onion (170g), chopped finely
2 fresh red thai chillies, chopped finely
⅓ cup coarsely chopped fresh coriander
4 x 200g mahi mahi steaks

1 Cook corn on heated oiled grill plate (or grill or barbecue) until browned lightly and just tender.
2 Meanwhile, blend or process yolk, garlic, juice and mustard until smooth. With motor operating, gradually add oil in a thin, steady stream; process until mayonnaise thickens slightly.
3 Using sharp knife, remove kernels from cobs. Place kernels in large bowl with onion, chilli, coriander and half of the mayonnaise; toss gently to combine.
4 Cook fish on heated oiled grill plate (or grill or barbecue) until browned both sides and cooked as desired. Divide corn salad among serving plates; top with fish, drizzle with remaining mayonnaise.

serves 4
per serving 53g fat; 4004kJ (957 cal)

TIPS Swordfish or red emperor can be used in place of mahi mahi, if desired. This corn and chilli salad goes well with Mexican food too – use it to accompany beef fajitas or bean and cheese burritos.

smoked trout and crisp noodle salad

PREPARATION TIME 25 MINUTES

Filleted portions of smoked trout, in a variety of sizes, are now available at most supermarkets; we used three 150g portions for this recipe. Fried noodles are crisp wheat noodles packaged (commonly in 100g packets) already deep-fried. You need a quarter of a medium red cabbage, about 375g, for this recipe.

450g smoked ocean trout fillets
3½ cups (280g) finely shredded red cabbage
2 medium carrots (240g), grated coarsely
2 x 100g packets fried noodles
4 green onions, sliced thinly
2 tablespoons toasted sesame seeds
½ cup (125ml) sweet chilli sauce
1 tablespoon sesame oil
2 tablespoons white wine vinegar
2 tablespoons soy sauce

1 Discard any skin and bones from fish. Flake fish in large bowl; add cabbage, carrot, noodles, onion and seeds.
2 Place remaining ingredients in screw-top jar; shake well. Drizzle dressing over salad; toss gently to combine.

serves 4
per serving 19.4g fat; 1701kJ (406 cal)

salmon in creamy lime fettuccine

PREPARATION TIME 20 MINUTES **COOKING TIME** 25 MINUTES

375g fettuccine
1 tablespoon olive oil
4 x 220g salmon fillets, skinned
1 small brown onion (80g), chopped finely
1 clove garlic, crushed
2 teaspoons finely grated lime rind
1 tablespoon lime juice
¼ cup (60ml) dry white wine
300ml cream
½ teaspoon drained pink peppercorns, crushed
⅓ cup coarsely chopped fresh chives

1 Cook pasta in large saucepan of boiling water, uncovered, until just tender.
2 Meanwhile, heat half of the oil in large non-stick frying pan; cook fish, uncovered, until browned both sides and cooked as desired. Place fish in large bowl; flake fish into large pieces.
3 Heat remaining oil in same pan; cook onion and garlic, stirring, until onion softens. Add rind, juice and wine; bring to a boil. Boil, stirring, until liquid reduces to about 2 tablespoons. Stir in cream and peppercorns; bring to a boil. Remove from heat.
4 Combine drained pasta and chives in bowl with fish, drizzle with sauce; toss gently to combine.

serves 4
per serving 53.9g fat; 4181kJ (999 cal)

TIPS Use tweezers to remove any pieces of bone from salmon.
Substitute black or green peppercorns, if you prefer.

smoked cod chowder

PREPARATION TIME 25 MINUTES **COOKING TIME** 45 MINUTES

We used desiree potatoes in this recipe.

600g smoked cod fillets
1 litre (4 cups) milk
2 bay leaves
8 black peppercorns
2 bacon rashers (140g), rind removed, chopped finely
40g butter
1 medium leek (350g), sliced thinly
1 tablespoon plain flour
1 cup (250ml) dry white wine
4 medium potatoes (800g), cut into 2cm cubes
300ml cream
2 tablespoons coarsely chopped fresh flat-leaf parsley

1 Place fish in large heavy-based frying pan. Pour half of the milk over fish; heat almost to a boil. Drain fish; discard milk. Return fish to pan with remaining milk, bay leaves and peppercorns; heat almost to a boil. Drain over large bowl; reserve milk and fish, discard bay leaves and peppercorns.
2 Cook bacon in same cleaned heated pan, stirring, until browned and crisp; drain on absorbent paper.
3 Melt butter in same cleaned pan; cook leek, stirring, until softened. Add flour; cook, stirring, until mixture thickens and bubbles. Gradually add wine; stir until mixture boils and thickens. Add potato and reserved milk, reduce heat; simmer, uncovered, stirring occasionally, about 20 minutes or until potato is tender.
4 Meanwhile, discard skin and bones from fish. Flake fish into large pieces, add to chowder with cream; cook, stirring gently, until heated through. Remove from heat; stir in parsley. Serve bowls of chowder sprinkled with bacon and accompanied by warm sourdough rolls, if desired.

serves 4
per serving 49.6g fat; 3330kJ (796 cal)

TIP Cooking the fish twice in milk helps remove the excess salt and tenderise the flesh.

salt and pepper salmon cutlets with daikon and snow pea salad

PREPARATION TIME 25 MINUTES **COOKING TIME** 10 MINUTES

Daikon, also known as white radish, is used extensively in Japanese cooking. Thai basil, also known as horapa, is available from Asian grocery stores and some specialist greengrocers.

2 teaspoons sea salt

1 teaspoon freshly ground black pepper

4 x 265g salmon cutlets

1 tablespoon peanut oil

½ small daikon (200g)

150g snow pea sprouts

200g snow peas, sliced thinly

1 fresh long red chilli, seeded, sliced thinly

½ cup loosely packed fresh thai basil leaves

½ cup loosely packed fresh vietnamese mint leaves

2 small pink grapefruit (460g)

CHILLI LIME VINAIGRETTE

2 tablespoons sweet chilli sauce

2 tablespoons lime juice

1 tablespoon rice vinegar

1 tablespoon finely chopped fresh lemon grass

1 clove garlic, crushed

2 teaspoons brown sugar

1 Make chilli lime vinaigrette.
2 Combine salt and pepper in large bowl, add fish; toss gently to coat in mixture. Heat oil in large frying pan; cook fish, in batches, until browned both sides and cooked as desired.
3 Meanwhile, slice daikon thinly lengthways; cut slices into thin sticks. Combine daikon in large bowl with sprouts, snow peas, chilli and herbs.
4 Segment grapefruit over salad to save juice; discard membranes from segments. Add segments and half of the vinaigrette to salad; toss gently to combine. Divide salad among serving plates; top with fish, drizzle with remaining vinaigrette.
CHILLI LIME VINAIGRETTE Place ingredients in screw-top jar; shake well.

serves 4
per serving 20.8g fat; 1925kJ (460 cal)

TIP If vietnamese mint is unavailable, use ordinary garden mint.

hot-smoked trout and vermicelli salad

PREPARATION TIME 25 MINUTES **COOKING TIME** 5 MINUTES

We used two hot-smoked ocean trout portions, weighing approximately 200g each, that were spiced with a blackening mixture of mountain pepper, native pepperberry, aniseed myrtle, salt and other flavourings before being "cooked" in hot smoking ovens. You can also use ordinary cold-smoked trout if hot-smoked trout is unavailable.

200g rice vermicelli
400g hot-smoked trout fillets
2 trimmed celery sticks (150g), sliced thinly
2 lebanese cucumbers (260g), seeded, sliced thinly
½ cup (75g) toasted shelled pistachios
¼ cup coarsely chopped fresh mint
¼ cup coarsely chopped fresh thai basil
⅓ cup (80ml) lime juice
1 teaspoon chilli oil
1 tablespoon sesame oil
2 tablespoons fish sauce
1 clove garlic, crushed

1 Place vermicelli in large heatproof bowl; cover with boiling water. Stand until just tender; drain. Rinse noodles under cold water; drain.
2 Meanwhile, discard skin and bones from fish. Flake fish into large pieces in large bowl; add noodles, celery, cucumber, nuts and herbs.
3 Place remaining ingredients in screw-top jar; shake well. Drizzle dressing over salad; toss gently to combine.

serves 4
per serving 20.5g fat; 2095kJ (501 cal)

TIPS Add more chilli oil to the dressing if you want to make the salad hotter, or use a finely chopped fresh chilli if chilli oil is unavailable.
The vermicelli can be soaked and drained several hours ahead; keep it in the refrigerator, covered, until you're ready to assemble the salad.

char-grilled swordfish with roasted mediterranean vegetables

PREPARATION TIME 20 MINUTES **COOKING TIME** 25 MINUTES

1 medium red capsicum (200g), sliced thickly
1 medium yellow capsicum (200g), sliced thickly
1 medium eggplant (300g), sliced thickly
2 large zucchini (300g), sliced thickly
½ cup (125ml) olive oil
250g cherry tomatoes
¼ cup (60ml) balsamic vinegar
1 clove garlic, crushed
2 teaspoons sugar
4 x 220g swordfish steaks
¼ cup coarsely chopped fresh basil

1 Preheat oven to hot.
2 Combine capsicums, eggplant and zucchini with 2 tablespoons of
the oil in large baking dish; roast, uncovered, in hot oven 15 minutes.
Add tomatoes; roast, uncovered, about 5 minutes or until vegetables
are just tender.
3 Meanwhile, combine remaining oil, vinegar, garlic and sugar in
screw-top jar; shake well. Brush a third of the dressing over fish;
cook fish, in batches, on heated oiled grill plate (or grill or barbecue)
until browned both sides and cooked as desired.
4 Combine vegetables in large bowl with basil and remaining dressing; toss
gently to combine. Divide vegetables among serving plates; top with fish.

serves 4
per serving 35.2g fat; 2300kJ (549 cal)

seared tuna with kipfler smash and salsa verde

PREPARATION TIME 25 MINUTES **COOKING TIME** 20 MINUTES

If the kipfler potatoes that you purchase for this recipe are young and quite small, scrubbing (rather than peeling) them well will be sufficient. Tuna is at its best if browned both sides but still fairly rare in the middle; overcooking will make it dry.

1kg kipfler potatoes, peeled, halved
30g butter
1 tablespoon extra virgin olive oil
4 x 175g tuna steaks
80g baby rocket leaves

SALSA VERDE
½ cup firmly packed fresh flat-leaf parsley leaves
¼ cup loosely packed fresh mint leaves
⅔ cup (160ml) extra virgin olive oil
¼ cup (50g) drained capers, rinsed
2 teaspoons dijon mustard
2 tablespoons lemon juice
8 anchovy fillets, drained
1 clove garlic, quartered

1 Boil, steam or microwave potato until tender; drain. Using potato masher, crush potato roughly in large bowl with butter and oil. Cover to keep warm.
2 Meanwhile, make salsa verde.
3 Cook fish, in batches, on heated oiled grill plate (or grill or barbecue) until browned both sides and cooked as desired.
4 Divide rocket and potato among serving plates; top with fish, drizzle with salsa verde.
   SALSA VERDE Blend or process ingredients until just combined. Transfer to medium jug; whisk before pouring over fish.

serves 4
per serving 61.4g fat; 3784kJ (904 cal)

red emperor in thai-style coconut sauce

PREPARATION TIME 20 MINUTES **COOKING TIME** 25 MINUTES

1½ cups (300g) jasmine rice
3¼ cups (800ml) coconut milk
4 kaffir lime leaves, sliced thinly
2 fresh red thai chillies, sliced thinly
4cm piece fresh ginger (20g), chopped finely
1 tablespoon fish sauce
2 tablespoons lime juice
1 tablespoon finely chopped fresh coriander root
1 tablespoon finely chopped fresh lemon grass
1 tablespoon grated palm sugar
2 x 440g red emperor fillets, skinned
⅓ cup firmly packed fresh coriander leaves

1 Cook rice in large saucepan of boiling water, uncovered, until just tender; drain.
2 Meanwhile, combine coconut milk, lime leaves, chilli, ginger, sauce, juice, coriander root, lemon grass and sugar in large frying pan; bring to a boil. Reduce heat; simmer, uncovered, 10 minutes. Add fish; simmer, covered, about 10 minutes or until fish is cooked through. Remove from heat; stir in coriander. Serve fish with coconut sauce on rice.

serves 4
per serving 46.7g fat; 3855kJ (921 cal)

TIP Any other firm white fish fillet, such as ling or perch, can be used in this recipe; cooking times will vary, depending on the fish used.

char-grilled bream and vegetables with chilli basil butter sauce

PREPARATION TIME 20 MINUTES **COOKING TIME** 30 MINUTES

4 baby cauliflowers (500g), halved
2 trimmed corn cobs (500g), cut into 2cm rounds
400g baby carrots, trimmed
2 tablespoons olive oil
4 x 240g whole bream

CHILLI BASIL BUTTER SAUCE
80g butter
2 fresh red thai chillies, seeded, chopped finely
⅓ cup firmly packed fresh basil leaves, shredded finely
1 tablespoon lemon juice

1 Place vegetables and half of the oil in large bowl; toss to combine. Cook vegetables on heated oiled grill plate (or grill or barbecue) about 20 minutes or until browned all over and cooked through.
2 Meanwhile, make chilli basil butter sauce.
3 Score each fish three times both sides; brush all over with remaining oil. Cook fish on heated oiled grill plate (or grill or barbecue) about 5 minutes each side or until cooked as desired. Serve fish and vegetables drizzled with sauce.
CHILLI BASIL BUTTER SAUCE Melt butter in small saucepan; add chilli, basil and juice, stir until combined.

serves 4
per serving 33.8g fat; 2185kJ (522 cal)

TIP Substitute bream fillets for whole bream, if desired.

sweet and spicy mussels
with stir-fried asian greens

PREPARATION TIME 20 MINUTES **COOKING TIME** 15 MINUTES

1kg large black mussels
1 tablespoon peanut oil
1 clove garlic, crushed
8cm piece fresh ginger (40g), chopped finely
⅓ cup (80ml) pure maple syrup
2 tablespoons soy sauce
1 tablespoon oyster sauce
¼ cup (60ml) fish stock
1 tablespoon lemon juice
4 green onions, sliced thinly
300g baby bok choy, chopped coarsely
400g gai larn, chopped coarsely
2 cups (160g) bean sprouts

1 Scrub mussels; remove beards.
2 Heat oil in wok or large frying pan; stir-fry garlic and ginger until fragrant. Add syrup, sauces, stock and juice; bring to a boil. Add mussels; return to a boil. Reduce heat; simmer, covered, about 5 minutes or until mussels open (discard any that do not). Remove mussels; cover to keep warm.
3 Return stock mixture to a boil. Add remaining ingredients to wok; stir-fry until greens are just wilted. Return mussels to wok; stir-fry until heated through. Accompany with steamed jasmine rice, if desired.

serves 4
per serving 6.4g fat; 836kJ (200 cal)

TIP Use a stiff brush to scrub the mussels under cold water.

grilled leatherjacket, sumac-roasted tomatoes and potato wedges

PREPARATION TIME 20 MINUTES **COOKING TIME** 30 MINUTES

Ask your seafood shop to sell you skinned leatherjackets. You can substitute the broccolini with any green vegetable you prefer.

1kg tiny new potatoes
1 tablespoon olive oil
500g cherry tomatoes, halved
2 teaspoons sumac
4 x 200g leatherjackets
80g butter
2 tablespoons lemon juice
1 clove garlic, crushed
500g broccolini, trimmed

1 Preheat oven to hot.
2 Cut potatoes into wedges; combine with oil on oven tray. Roast, uncovered, in hot oven, turning occasionally, about 25 minutes or until browned and crisp.
3 Meanwhile, place tomato, cut-side up, on lightly oiled oven tray; sprinkle with sumac. Roast, uncovered, in hot oven with wedges about 10 minutes or until softened.
4 Cook fish on heated oiled grill plate (or grill or barbecue) until browned both sides and cooked as desired.
5 Heat butter, juice and garlic in small saucepan; stir until butter melts.
6 Meanwhile, boil, steam or microwave broccolini until just tender; drain.
7 Divide fish, potato, tomato and broccolini among serving plates; drizzle with butter sauce.

serves 4
per serving 22.6g fat; 2011kJ (480 cal)

TIP Sumac is a purple-red, astringent spice that adds a lemony flavour to foods; it is available from Middle-Eastern food stores and some supermarkets.

moroccan blue-eye fillets with fruity couscous

PREPARATION TIME 20 MINUTES **COOKING TIME** 15 MINUTES

1 clove garlic, crushed
1cm piece fresh ginger (5g), grated finely
1 teaspoon ground cumin
½ teaspoon ground turmeric
½ teaspoon hot paprika
½ teaspoon ground coriander
4 x 200g blue-eye fillets, skinned
1 tablespoon olive oil

FRUITY COUSCOUS
2 cups (400g) couscous
2 cups (500ml) boiling water
50g butter
1 large pear (330g), chopped finely
½ cup (75g) finely chopped dried apricots
½ cup (95g) coarsely chopped dried figs
½ cup coarsely chopped fresh flat-leaf parsley
¼ cup (40g) toasted pine nuts

1 Combine garlic, ginger and spices in large bowl. Add fish; toss to coat fish in spice mixture. Heat oil in large frying pan; cook fish, in batches, until browned both sides and cooked as desired.
2 Meanwhile, make fruity couscous.
3 Divide couscous among serving plates; top with fish. Accompany with a bowl of combined yogurt and coarsely chopped fresh coriander, if desired.
   FRUITY COUSCOUS Combine couscous, the water and butter in large heatproof bowl, cover; stand about 5 minutes or until water is absorbed, fluffing with fork occasionally. Stir in remaining ingredients.

serves 4
per serving 27.5g fat; 3816kJ (912 cal)

blue-eye cutlets with mango salsa

PREPARATION TIME 25 MINUTES **COOKING TIME** 15 MINUTES

4 x 200g blue-eye cutlets
2 tablespoons lime juice
1 tablespoon fish sauce
1 tablespoon peanut oil
1 tablespoon grated palm sugar
1 teaspoon sambal oelek
2 kaffir lime leaves, shredded finely

MANGO SALSA
2 large mangoes (1.2kg), chopped coarsely
2 lebanese cucumbers (260g), seeded, chopped coarsely
1 fresh long red chilli, seeded, sliced thinly
½ cup coarsely chopped fresh mint

1 Make mango salsa.
2 Cook fish, in batches, on heated oiled grill plate (or grill or barbecue) until browned both sides and cooked as desired.
3 Place remaining ingredients in screw-top jar; shake well. Divide salsa and fish among serving plates; drizzle with dressing.
MANGO SALSA Place ingredients in medium bowl; toss gently to combine.

serves 4
per serving 8.8g fat; 1481kJ (354 cal)

prawn and kingfish skewers with coconut rice

PREPARATION TIME 25 MINUTES **COOKING TIME** 25 MINUTES

You need to soak 8 bamboo skewers in water for at least an hour before using to prevent them splintering and scorching.

16 uncooked large king prawns (1.1kg)
4 x 300g kingfish fillets
1 tablespoon ground cumin
2 teaspoons ground coriander
½ teaspoon chilli powder
¼ cup (60ml) peanut oil
2 teaspoons fish sauce
2 teaspoons lime juice

COCONUT RICE
1¾ cups (350g) white long-grain rice
1⅔ cups (400ml) coconut cream
2¼ cups (560ml) water
⅓ cup (15g) flaked coconut
¾ cup loosely packed fresh coriander leaves

1 Make coconut rice.
2 Shell and devein prawns, leaving tails intact. Cut each fillet into six pieces. Thread alternate pieces of fish and prawns on skewers.
3 Combine spices, oil, sauce and juice in small bowl; brush over fish and prawns. Cook skewers on heated oiled grill plate (or grill or barbecue) until browned all over and cooked as desired. Serve skewers with coconut rice.
COCONUT RICE Combine rice, coconut cream and the water in large heavy-based saucepan; bring to a boil, stirring occasionally. Reduce heat; simmer, covered, about 20 minutes or until liquid is absorbed and rice is just tender. Meanwhile, heat dry small frying pan; cook flaked coconut, stirring, over low heat, until browned lightly. Stir toasted coconut and coriander into rice.

serves 4
per serving 45.7g fat; 4629kJ (1106 cal)

prawn laksa

PREPARATION TIME 15 MINUTES **COOKING TIME** 30 MINUTES

1kg uncooked large king prawns
⅔ cup (180g) laksa paste
3¼ cups (800ml) coconut milk
1 litre (4 cups) chicken stock
1½ cups (375ml) fish stock
1 fresh long red chilli, sliced thinly
6 kaffir lime leaves, shredded finely
250g rice stick noodles
3 cups (240g) bean sprouts
6 green onions, sliced thinly
1 cup (150g) toasted unsalted cashews
½ cup loosely packed fresh coriander leaves

1 Shell and devein prawns, leaving tails intact.
2 Cook paste in large heated saucepan, stirring, until fragrant.
   Stir in coconut milk, stocks, chilli and lime leaves; bring to a
   boil. Reduce heat; simmer, covered, 20 minutes.
3 Add prawns to laksa mixture; simmer, uncovered, about
   5 minutes or until prawns just change in colour.
4 Meanwhile, place noodles in large heatproof bowl; cover with
   boiling water. Stand until just tender; drain.
5 Divide noodles among serving bowls. Ladle laksa mixture over
   noodles; top with sprouts, onion, cashews then coriander.

serves 4
per serving 72.1g fat; 5094kJ (1217 cal)

TIP Tofu can be added to this recipe, if desired. Stir cubes of
firm tofu into laksa mixture just before serving.

fettuccine alle vongole

PREPARATION TIME 15 MINUTES **COOKING TIME** 15 MINUTES

A classic pasta vongole is made with tiny baby clams in Italy, but you can use a mixture of any available bivalves for this recipe.

2 tablespoons olive oil
3 cloves garlic, crushed
1 fresh long red chilli, chopped finely
1 tablespoon drained baby capers, rinsed
¾ cup (180ml) dry white wine
¾ cup (180ml) fish stock
2 tablespoons lemon juice
1kg clams
375g fettuccine
½ cup coarsely chopped fresh flat-leaf parsley
¼ cup coarsely chopped fresh chives

1   Heat oil in large saucepan; cook garlic and chilli, stirring, 1 minute. Add capers, wine, stock and juice; bring to a boil. Add clams; cook vongole mixture, covered, about 5 minutes or until clams open (discard any that do not).
2   Meanwhile, cook pasta in large saucepan of boiling water, uncovered, until just tender; drain.
3   Add pasta with herbs to vongole mixture; toss gently to combine.

serves 4
per serving 11.3g fat; 2068kJ (494 cal)

whiting parcels with porcini and sun-dried tomatoes on soft polenta

PREPARATION TIME 20 MINUTES (PLUS STANDING TIME) **COOKING TIME** 20 MINUTES

A modern take on the traditional method of cooking "en papillote" (in sealed packets), this recipe uses aluminium foil rather than parchment paper to enclose the ingredients. Cooking this way reduces the need for any added fat and allows the flavours to mingle and intensify. Aromatic, earthy-flavoured porcini mushrooms (also known as cèpes) are available both fresh and dried; the latter are reconstituted and used in many classic Italian dishes, such as various risottos and pasta sauces.

30g dried porcini mushrooms
30g butter, melted
1 clove garlic, crushed
½ cup (75g) drained sun-dried tomatoes in oil, chopped coarsely
2 tablespoons finely shredded fresh sage leaves
8 x 120g whiting fillets, with skin
2 tablespoons lemon juice

SOFT POLENTA
2 cups (500ml) chicken stock
2 cups (500ml) milk
1 cup (250ml) water
1 cup (170g) polenta
⅓ cup (25g) coarsely grated parmesan cheese

1 Place mushrooms in small heatproof bowl, cover with boiling water; stand 20 minutes. Drain; chop coarsely. Combine butter and garlic in medium bowl; add mushroom, tomato and sage, stir to combine.
2 Preheat oven to hot.
3 Centre four of the fillets, skin-side down, on four 60cm-pieces of lightly oiled foil; top each fillet with equal amounts of the mushroom mixture. Top with remaining fillets, skin-side up; drizzle with juice. Gather corners of foil together above fillets; twist to enclose securely.
4 Place parcels on oven tray; bake in hot oven about 15 minutes or until fish is cooked as desired.
5 Meanwhile, make soft polenta.
6 Discard foil from parcels just before serving on polenta.
SOFT POLENTA Bring stock, milk and the water to a boil in medium saucepan. Gradually add polenta; cook, stirring, about 5 minutes or until polenta thickens. Stir in cheese.

serves 4
per serving 17.6g fat; 2430kJ (580 cal)

ling and snow pea green curry

PREPARATION TIME 30 MINUTES **COOKING TIME** 15 MINUTES

1¼ cups (250g) jasmine rice
2 teaspoons peanut oil
1 medium brown onion (150g), chopped finely
3 fresh small green chillies, seeded, sliced thinly
¼ cup (75g) green curry paste
1⅔ cups (400ml) coconut milk
4 x 200g ling fillets, skinned, chopped coarsely
200g snow peas, halved
4 green onions, sliced thinly
¼ cup coarsely chopped fresh coriander

1 Cook rice in large saucepan of boiling water, uncovered, until tender;
   drain. Cover to keep warm.
2 Meanwhile, heat oil in large saucepan; cook brown onion, chilli and
   curry paste, stirring, until onion softens. Stir in coconut milk; bring to a
   boil. Add fish, reduce heat; simmer, uncovered, 5 minutes. Add snow
   peas and green onion; stir gently until vegetables are just tender.
   Remove from heat; stir in half of the coriander. Serve curry with rice;
   sprinkle with remaining coriander.

serves 4
per serving 27.9g fat; 2839kJ (678 cal)

fish fingers with potato and pea mash

PREPARATION TIME 35 MINUTES **COOKING TIME** 20 MINUTES

1kg ling fillets, skinned, chopped coarsely
2 tablespoons coarsely chopped fresh chives
1 teaspoon curry powder
½ cup (75g) plain flour
2 eggs, beaten lightly
2 tablespoons milk
⅔ cup (70g) packaged breadcrumbs
⅔ cup (60g) desiccated coconut
vegetable oil, for shallow-frying

POTATO AND PEA MASH
1kg potatoes, chopped coarsely
1 cup (125g) frozen peas
40g butter
½ cup (125ml) milk

1 Grease 19cm x 29cm slice pan.
2 Process fish, chives and curry powder, pulsing, until mixture forms a smooth paste. Using spatula, press mixture evenly into prepared pan; turn onto baking-paper-lined tray. Cut into eight 19cm slices; cut each slice in half to make 16 fingers.
3 Pat fish fingers with flour, shaking away excess carefully; dip into combined egg and milk then in combined breadcrumbs and coconut.
4 Heat oil in large frying pan; shallow-fry fish fingers, in batches, until browned lightly and cooked through. Drain on absorbent paper.
5 Meanwhile, make potato and pea mash. Serve with fish fingers.
POTATO AND PEA MASH Boil, steam or microwave potato and peas, separately, until tender; drain. Mash potato in large bowl with butter and milk until smooth. Mash peas in small bowl until crushed. Add peas to potato mash; using wooden spoon, gently marble peas through potato.

serves 4
per serving 61.5g fat; 4400kJ (1051 cal)

baby octopus and eggplant in tomato and caper sauce

PREPARATION TIME 10 MINUTES **COOKING TIME** 25 MINUTES

Shallots, also called french shallots, golden shallots or eschalots, are small, elongated members of the onion family that grow in tight clusters similar to garlic.

1 tablespoon olive oil
1.2kg whole cleaned baby octopus
1 clove garlic, sliced thinly
3 shallots (45g), sliced thinly
4 baby eggplants (240g), sliced thinly
1 medium red capsicum (200g), sliced thinly
½ cup (125ml) dry red wine
700g bottled tomato pasta sauce
⅓ cup (80ml) water
¼ cup (40g) drained baby capers, rinsed
2 tablespoons coarsely chopped fresh oregano

1 Heat half of the oil in large deep frying pan; cook octopus, in batches, until just changed in colour and tender. Cover to keep warm.
2 Heat remaining oil in same pan; cook garlic and shallot, stirring, until shallot softens. Add eggplant and capsicum; cook, stirring, about 5 minutes or until vegetables are just tender.
3 Add wine, sauce, the water and octopus; bring to a boil. Reduce heat; simmer, covered, about 10 minutes or until sauce thickens slightly. Stir in capers and oregano. Top with extra oregano leaves and serve with steamed white long-grain rice, if desired.

serves 4
per serving 8g fat; 1281kJ (306 cal)

steamed scallops with asian flavours

PREPARATION TIME 15 MINUTES **COOKING TIME** 15 MINUTES

1½ cups (300g) jasmine rice
3cm piece fresh ginger (15g)
20 scallops (800g), in half shell, roe removed
2 tablespoons thinly sliced fresh lemon grass
4 green onions, sliced thinly
1 tablespoon sesame oil
¼ cup (60ml) kecap manis
¼ cup (60ml) soy sauce

1 Cook rice in large saucepan of boiling water, uncovered, until just tender; drain.
2 Meanwhile, slice ginger thinly; cut slices into thin strips. Place scallops, in batches, in single layer in large bamboo steamer; top with ginger, lemon grass and onion. Cover then steam scallops about 5 minutes or until tender and cooked as desired.
3 Divide scallops among serving plates; top scallops with combined remaining ingredients. Serve with rice.

serves 4
per serving 5.6g fat; 1509kJ (361 cal)

TIP You can also use scallops with the roe attached, if you prefer.

grilled snapper fillets with fennel and onion salad

PREPARATION TIME 15 MINUTES **COOKING TIME** 10 MINUTES

1 medium red onion (170g), sliced thinly
4 green onions, sliced thinly
1 large fennel (550g), trimmed, sliced thinly
2 trimmed celery sticks (150g), sliced thinly
½ cup coarsely chopped fresh flat-leaf parsley
⅓ cup (80ml) orange juice
¼ cup (60ml) olive oil
2 cloves garlic, crushed
2 teaspoons sambal oelek
4 x 275g snapper fillets, with skin

1 Combine onions, fennel, celery and parsley in medium bowl.
2 Place juice, oil, garlic and sambal in screw-top jar; shake well.
3 Cook fish on heated oiled grill plate (or grill or barbecue) until browned both sides and cooked as desired.
4 Pour half of the dressing over salad in bowl; toss gently to combine. Serve salad topped with fish; drizzle with remaining dressing.

serves 4
per serving 18.9g fat; 1813kJ (433 cal)

crab and apple salad

PREPARATION TIME 20 MINUTES **COOKING TIME** 5 MINUTES

250g sugar snap peas, trimmed
1 large apple (200g)
500g cooked blue swimmer crab meat
1 medium red onion (170g), halved, sliced thinly
2 fresh red thai chillies, seeded, sliced thinly lengthways
2 medium avocados (500g), sliced thickly
150g mesclun
⅓ cup (80ml) olive oil
¼ cup (60ml) lemon juice
1 tablespoon dijon mustard
1 clove garlic, crushed

1 Boil, steam or microwave peas until just tender; drain. Rinse under cold water; drain.
2 Slice apple thinly; cut slices into thin strips. Combine peas and apple in large bowl with crab, onion, chilli, avocado and mesclun.
3 Place remaining ingredients in screw-top jar; shake well. Drizzle dressing over salad; toss gently to combine.

serves 4
per serving 40.1g fat; 2094kJ (500 cal)

blue-eye fillet, baby leek and fennel parcels with fried cauliflower

PREPARATION TIME 20 MINUTES **COOKING TIME** 15 MINUTES

A modern take on the traditional method of cooking "en papillote" (in sealed packets), this recipe uses aluminium foil rather than parchment paper to enclose the ingredients. Cooking this way allows the flavours to mingle and intensify.

4 x 200g blue-eye fillets, with skin
½ medium fennel (150g), trimmed, sliced thinly
4 baby leeks (320g), quartered lengthways
30g butter, melted
vegetable oil, for deep-frying
1 medium cauliflower (1.5kg), cut into florets

1 Preheat oven to hot.
2 Place each fillet on a square of lightly oiled foil large enough to completely enclose fish; top each fillet with a quarter of the fennel and a quarter of the leek, drizzle with butter. Gather corners of foil squares together above fish; twist to enclose securely.
3 Place parcels on oven tray; bake in hot oven about 15 minutes or until fish is cooked as desired.
4 Meanwhile, heat oil in wok or large frying pan; deep-fry cauliflower, in batches, until browned and crisp. Drain on absorbent paper.
5 Discard foil from parcels just before serving on cauliflower.

serves 4
per serving 30.6g fat; 2140kJ (511 cal)

TIP When deep-frying the cauliflower, make sure the oil is very hot so the vegetable crisps and browns. If not, the cauliflower will absorb excess oil and become limp and soggy.

pick an oyster

We've done a combination of both cooked and uncooked oysters to suit anyone's tastebuds.
All recipes make 12 and can be prepared in under 30 minutes.

japanese oysters with shiitake mushrooms

Combine 1 tablespoon sake,
2 tablespoons mirin, 1 tablespoon
rice vinegar and 1 tablespoon
tamari in small jug. Heat 1 tablespoon
sesame oil in small frying pan;
cook 100g thinly sliced fresh
shiitake mushrooms, stirring, until
tender. Add half of the sake mixture;
cook, stirring, until liquid is absorbed.
Divide mushroom mixture evenly
among 12 oysters on the half shell;
spoon remaining sake mixture over
oysters. Serve oysters topped with
2 thinly sliced green onions.
per oyster 1.8g fat; 131kJ (31 cal)

garlic and fennel cream oysters

Melt 20g butter in small frying pan;
cook 1 small thinly sliced fennel and
1 clove crushed garlic, stirring, about
5 minutes or until fennel is tender.
Add 2 tablespoons dry white wine;
cook, stirring, until wine evaporates.
Stir in ⅓ cup cream; cook, stirring,
until mixture thickens. Stir in
1 tablespoon finely chopped drained
capers and 2 teaspoons finely
chopped fresh flat-leaf parsley.
Divide fennel mixture among
12 oysters on the half shell.
per oyster 4.5g fat; 212kJ (51 cal)

oysters with tomato, bacon and basil

Heat 1 tablespoon olive oil in small
frying pan; cook ½ small finely
chopped red onion and 1 clove
crushed garlic, stirring, until onion
softens. Add 2 finely chopped
rindless bacon rashers; cook,
stirring, until browned lightly. Add
2 medium finely chopped seeded
tomatoes; cook, stirring, until
tomato just softens. Stir in
1 tablespoon finely shredded fresh
basil. Place 12 oysters on the half
shell on oven tray; divide tomato
mixture among oysters, top each
with 1 teaspoon finely grated
parmesan cheese. Place under
hot grill until cheese melts and
is browned lightly.
per oyster 3.2g fat; 183kJ (44 cal)

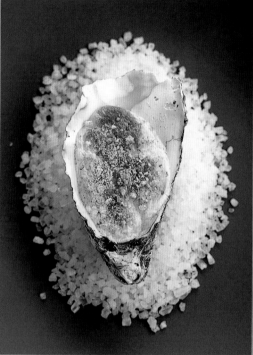

mexican-style fried oysters

Preheat oven to moderate. Combine 1 small finely chopped tomato, ½ finely chopped yellow capsicum, ½ medium finely chopped red onion, 1 tablespoon finely chopped fresh coriander, 1 tablespoon olive oil, 1 tablespoon lime juice and 1 fresh finely chopped seeded red thai chilli in small bowl. Remove 12 oysters from shells; reserve oysters. Place shells on oven tray; heat in moderate oven 5 minutes. Combine ½ cup polenta, ⅓ cup milk, 1 beaten egg and pinch cayenne pepper in small bowl. Heat vegetable oil in medium saucepan, dip oysters in batter; deep-fry until browned lightly. Drain on absorbent paper. Return oysters to shells; top with salsa.
per oyster 5.7g fat; 361kJ (86 cal)

cheese and chive souffléd oysters

Preheat oven to hot. Melt 20g butter in small saucepan; cook 2 teaspoons plain flour, stirring, until mixture thickens and bubbles. Gradually add ¼ cup milk; stir until mixture boils and thickens. Remove from heat; stir in 1 egg yolk, 2 tablespoons finely grated parmesan cheese and 1 tablespoon finely chopped fresh chives. Beat 1 egg white in small bowl with electric mixer until soft peaks form; gently fold into yolk mixture. Place 12 oysters on the half shell on oven tray. Top oysters with soufflé mixture; sprinkle with combined 1 tablespoon stale breadcrumbs and ¼ teaspoon sweet paprika. Bake in hot oven about 5 minutes or until puffed and browned lightly. Serve immediately.
per oyster 2.7g fat; 159kJ (38 cal)

oysters with salsa verde

Blend or process ⅓ cup coarsely chopped fresh flat-leaf parsley, 2 tablespoons coarsely chopped fresh mint, 2 teaspoons drained capers, 1 anchovy fillet, 1 quartered garlic clove, ½ teaspoon finely grated lemon rind, 1 teaspoon lemon juice and ½ teaspoon dijon mustard until chopped finely. With motor operating, gradually add ⅓ cup extra virgin olive oil in a thin, steady stream; process until mixture is almost smooth. Divide salsa verde among 12 oysters on the half shell; sprinkle ¼ teaspoon extra finely grated lemon rind over oysters.
per oyster 6.6g fat; 271kJ (65 cal)

The delicious recipes that follow are perfect for weekend entertaining, when you have more time to prepare a special dish for your family – or can indulge a love of cooking with a sumptuous dinner for friends.

char-grilled lobster tail salad

PREPARATION TIME 15 MINUTES **COOKING TIME** 20 MINUTES

4 uncooked small lobster tails in shell (800g)
2 radicchio (400g), trimmed, leaves separated
1 medium avocado (250g), chopped coarsely
4 radishes (140g), trimmed, sliced thinly
⅓ cup (50g) toasted pine nuts
4 green onions, sliced thinly
150g semi-dried tomatoes, drained, chopped coarsely

ROSEMARY VINAIGRETTE

⅓ cup (80ml) vegetable oil
¼ cup (60ml) red wine vinegar
1 tablespoon coarsely chopped fresh rosemary
1 tablespoon dijon mustard

1 Make rosemary vinaigrette.
2 Using kitchen scissors, discard soft shell from underneath lobster tails to expose meat; cook, in batches, on heated oiled grill plate (or grill or barbecue) until browned and cooked through, brushing with a third of the vinaigrette. Cut lobster tails in half lengthways.
3 Meanwhile, place remaining ingredients in large bowl with remaining vinaigrette; toss gently to combine. Serve lobster on salad.
ROSEMARY VINAIGRETTE Place ingredients in screw-top jar; shake well.

serves 4
per serving 41.3g fat; 2508kJ (600 cal)

tea-smoked salmon with broccolini and jasmine rice

PREPARATION TIME 15 MINUTES (PLUS REFRIGERATION TIME) **COOKING TIME** 20 MINUTES

Cooking over smouldering tea leaves in a covered wok is a form of "hot smoking", and salmon cooked this way will be more strongly flavoured than conventionally cold-smoked salmon. Any fish or meat can be smoked in this manner, but cooking times will differ. Additional requirements for this recipe are: clean, damp tea towels, aluminium foil, a large bamboo steamer… and a good extractor fan!

½ cup (125ml) water
½ cup (125ml) mirin
1 tablespoon brown sugar
1 tablespoon sea salt
4 x 200g salmon fillets, with skin
½ cup (110g) caster sugar
1 cup (65g) green tea leaves
2½ cups (500g) jasmine rice
350g broccolini, trimmed, halved
1 lemon, cut into 8 wedges

1 Combine the water, mirin, brown sugar and salt in medium bowl; stir to dissolve sugar. Add fish; stir to coat in mirin mixture. Cover; refrigerate 1 hour.
2 Meanwhile, line large wok with three layers of foil. Place caster sugar, tea and 1 cup of the jasmine rice on foil in wok; stir gently to combine.
3 Cook remaining rice in large saucepan of boiling water, uncovered, until just tender; drain. Cover to keep warm.
4 Meanwhile, discard marinade; place fish, in single layer, in large bamboo steamer. Turn heat to high under wok; when tea mixture starts to smoke, sit steamer over tea mixture. Cover steamer tightly; wind two dampened tea towels in gap between steamer and wok to contain smoke. Cook fish 10 minutes.
5 Boil, steam or microwave broccolini until just tender; drain. Serve fish with rice, broccolini and lemon wedges.

serves 4
per serving 14.8g fat; 2586kJ (618 cal)

When the tea mixture starts to smoulder, sit the steamer in the wok

Wrap two dampened tea towels in the gap between the steamer and the wok

flake vindaloo with chapatis

PREPARATION TIME 1 HOUR 20 MINUTES (PLUS REFRIGERATION TIME) **COOKING TIME** 45 MINUTES

Vindaloo, made distinctive by the use of vinegar, is a fairly hot curry traditionally made with pork. It originated in the then-Portuguese colony of Goa in western India, and the name is derived from the Portuguese words for vinegar and garlic. Flake is also called dogfish or gummy shark; you can substitute any other slightly firm white-fleshed fish but may have to adjust the cooking time. Dried ancho chillies (called poblano chillies when fresh) are fruity, sweet and quite smoky in flavour. They measure about 8cm in length and are a dark reddish-brown in colour. We have made extra vindaloo paste in this recipe for you to use in future recipes; it will keep, covered and frozen, for up to 3 months.

6 cloves garlic, unpeeled
1 medium brown onion (150g), unpeeled
15g small dried red chillies
30g dried ancho chillies
1 teaspoon black peppercorns
1 cinnamon stick
1½ teaspoons cumin seeds
1 teaspoon fennel seeds
5cm piece fresh ginger (25g), chopped coarsely
1 tablespoon tamarind concentrate
1 tablespoon grated palm sugar
⅔ cup (160ml) cider vinegar
1kg flake fillets, skinned, cut into 5cm cubes
1 cup (250ml) water

CHAPATIS
2½ cups (400g) wholemeal plain flour
1 tablespoon peanut oil
1 cup (250ml) warm water

1 Preheat oven to moderately hot.
2 Place garlic and onion in small oiled baking dish; roast, uncovered, in moderately hot oven for 20 minutes, adding combined chillies, peppercorns, cinnamon and seeds to dish for the last 2 minutes of roasting time. Reserve onion and garlic; blend or process remaining spice mixture until ground finely.
3 Peel garlic and onion; add to blender with ginger, tamarind, sugar and half of the vinegar; process until mixture forms a smooth paste. Combine ⅓ cup of the vindaloo paste and remaining vinegar with fish in large bowl; toss to coat fish. Cover; refrigerate 3 hours or overnight. Reserve remaining paste for future use.
4 Meanwhile, make chapati dough.
5 Combine fish mixture with the water in large saucepan; bring to a boil. Reduce heat; simmer, uncovered, about 15 minutes or until fish is cooked through.
6 Meanwhile, cook chapatis. Serve with fish, and raita (page 75), if desired.
   CHAPATIS Using hands, combine flour, oil and the water in large bowl; transfer to lightly floured surface, knead 10 minutes. Wrap in plastic, refrigerate about 3 hours. Knead dough for 1 minute; divide into 16 pieces, roll each piece into a ball. Roll balls to 15cm rounds; stack rounds between pieces of greaseproof paper and refrigerate until ready to cook. Just before serving, dry-fry chapatis, one at a time, on heated large non-stick griddle (or in frying pan) until puffed and cooked through.

serves 4
per serving 7.3g fat; 2691kJ (643 cal)

barbecued squid and octopus salad

PREPARATION TIME 30 MINUTES (PLUS REFRIGERATION TIME) **COOKING TIME** 10 MINUTES

600g squid hoods, cleaned
600g whole cleaned baby octopus
2 fresh long green chillies, chopped finely
6 cloves garlic, crushed
¼ cup (60ml) extra virgin olive oil
500g asparagus, halved
500g yellow teardrop tomatoes, halved lengthways
6 spring onions, trimmed, quartered lengthways
2 tablespoons coarsely chopped fresh flat-leaf parsley
200g cornichons, rinsed, drained
1 medium orange (240g), peeled, sliced thickly
80g baby spinach leaves

ORANGE VINAIGRETTE
⅓ cup (80ml) extra virgin olive oil
¼ cup (60ml) fresh orange juice
1 teaspoon finely grated orange rind
2 tablespoons malt vinegar

1 Cut squid down centre to open out; score inside in diagonal pattern then cut into thick strips. Quarter octopus lengthways.
2 Combine squid and octopus in large bowl with chilli, garlic and oil; toss to coat seafood in marinade. Cover; refrigerate 3 hours or overnight.
3 Make orange vinaigrette.
4 Boil, steam or microwave asparagus until just tender; drain. Rinse under cold water; drain. Combine in large bowl with remaining ingredients.
5 Drain seafood; cook, in batches, on heated oiled grill plate (or grill or barbecue) until browned lightly and cooked through. Place in bowl with salad, add vinaigrette; toss gently to combine.
   ORANGE VINAIGRETTE Combine ingredients in screw-top jar; shake well.

serves 4
per serving 36.4g fat; 2280kJ (545 cal)

pesto-topped grilled mussels with green onion polenta

PREPARATION TIME 25 MINUTES **COOKING TIME** 20 MINUTES

1kg large black mussels
½ cup (125ml) dry white wine
½ cup (125ml) water

ROCKET PESTO
70g rocket leaves
½ cup (55g) toasted walnuts
1 clove garlic, quartered
¼ cup (20g) coarsely grated parmesan cheese
2 teaspoons coarsely grated orange rind
½ cup (125ml) olive oil

GREEN ONION POLENTA
3 cups (750ml) water
2 cups (500ml) chicken stock
½ cup (125ml) orange juice
1 cup (170g) polenta
¼ cup (20g) finely grated parmesan cheese
8 green onions, sliced thinly

1 Scrub mussels; remove beards. Make rocket pesto.
2 Bring wine and the water to a boil in large saucepan. Add mussels; cook, covered, about 5 minutes or until mussels open (discard any that do not). Drain mussels; discard liquid. Break open shells; discard tops. Loosen mussels from shells with a spoon; place mussels, in half shells, in single layer on oven trays. Top each mussel with 1 teaspoon of the pesto.
3 Make green onion polenta. When polenta is almost cooked, place trays of mussels under preheated grill until pesto bubbles and browns lightly. Serve mussels on polenta.
ROCKET PESTO Blend or process rocket, nuts, garlic, cheese and rind until almost smooth. With motor operating, gradually add oil until pesto forms a smooth paste.
GREEN ONION POLENTA Bring the water, stock and juice to a boil in medium saucepan. Gradually add polenta; cook, stirring, about 5 minutes or until polenta thickens. Stir in cheese and onion.

serves 4
per serving 44.9g fat; 2671kJ (638 cal)

tuna tartare

PREPARATION TIME 45 MINUTES **COOKING TIME** 5 MINUTES

You need one small chinese cabbage weighing about 400g for this recipe.

200g green beans, halved
600g piece sashimi tuna
3 cups (240g) finely shredded chinese cabbage
4 green onions, sliced thinly
½ cup firmly packed fresh coriander leaves
2 cups (160g) bean sprouts

GINGER DRESSING
7cm piece fresh ginger (35g)
⅓ cup (80ml) lime juice
¼ cup (60ml) olive oil
1 tablespoon soy sauce
2 teaspoons finely chopped coriander root
2 cloves garlic, crushed
2 teaspoons sesame oil
2 teaspoons sugar

1 Boil, steam or microwave beans until just tender; drain. Rinse under cold water; drain.
2 Make ginger dressing.
3 Cut tuna into 5mm pieces. Place in medium bowl with a third of the dressing; toss gently to combine.
4 Place beans in large bowl with cabbage, onion, coriander, sprouts and remaining dressing; toss gently to combine.
5 Divide undrained tuna among serving plates, shaping into mound; serve with cabbage salad.
  GINGER DRESSING Cut ginger into thin slices; cut slices into thin strips. Combine ginger with remaining ingredients in small bowl.

serves 4
per serving 25.4g fat; 1751kJ (418 cal)

TIP Sashimi salmon can be used in place of the tuna.

vine-leaf-wrapped sardine fillets with dukkah

PREPARATION TIME 25 MINUTES **COOKING TIME** 20 MINUTES

Sardines can be purchased, butterflied, with bones and heads removed. Dukkah is an Egyptian nut, seed and spice mixture used to add an exotically complex flavour to grilled, fried or barbecued seafood or meat. Grapevine leaves in brine come cryovac-packed and can be found in most Middle-Eastern food stores.

24 butterflied sardines (1kg)
24 grapevine leaves in brine (100g), rinsed, drained
2 x 300g cans chickpeas, rinsed, drained
⅓ cup firmly packed fresh flat-leaf parsley leaves
¼ cup (45g) finely chopped preserved lemon rind
½ cup (40g) toasted flaked almonds
⅓ cup (80ml) olive oil
¼ cup (60ml) lemon juice
100g curly endive

DUKKAH
2 tablespoons hazelnut meal
1 tablespoon almond meal
1 tablespoon cumin seeds, crushed
1 tablespoon ground coriander
1 tablespoon sweet paprika
1 teaspoon sesame seeds
1 teaspoon black sesame seeds

1   Make dukkah.
2   Place fish, skin-side down, on board. Sprinkle about 1 teaspoon of the dukkah over one half of each fish; fold over other half to enclose. Wrap each sardine tightly in a vine leaf.
3   Cook fish, in batches, in lightly oiled large frying pan about 3 minutes each side or until cooked through.
4   Meanwhile, place remaining ingredients in large bowl; toss gently to combine. Serve fish with salad.
    DUKKAH   Heat dry medium frying pan; cook ingredients, stirring constantly, until mixture is fragrant.

serves 4
per serving 55.9g fat; 3013kJ (720 cal)

tuna, kingfish and salmon carpaccio

PREPARATION TIME 50 MINUTES (PLUS FREEZING AND REFRIGERATION TIMES)

350g piece sashimi tuna
350g piece sashimi kingfish
350g piece sashimi salmon
⅓ cup (80ml) lime juice
⅔ cup (160ml) lemon juice
4cm piece fresh ginger (20g), grated finely
¼ cup (60ml) soy sauce
1 baby fennel (130g)
⅓ cup (80ml) extra virgin olive oil
1 tablespoon drained baby capers, rinsed
½ small red onion (50g), sliced thinly
1 teaspoon finely chopped fresh dill

Buy the freshest fish you can because, while the citrus juice will change the colour and texture, the fish in this recipe is still raw when you eat it. You need approximately two limes and three lemons for this recipe.

1 Tightly wrap fish, separately, in plastic wrap; freeze about 1 hour or until slightly firm.
2 Unwrap fish then slice as thinly as possible. Arrange slices on separate serving platters; drizzle tuna with lime juice, drizzle kingfish and salmon with lemon juice. Cover platters; refrigerate 1 hour.
3 Meanwhile, combine ginger and sauce in small jug; stand while fish is under refrigeration. Finely chop enough fennel leaves to make 1 level tablespoon; discard remaining leaves. Chop fennel bulb finely.
4 Drain excess juice from platters. To serve, divide fish among serving plates: drizzle tuna with strained sauce mixture; sprinkle kingfish with fennel, leaves and half of the oil; sprinkle salmon with capers, onion, dill and remaining oil. Serve carpaccio with crusty bread, if desired.

serves 6
per serving 21.6g fat; 1522kJ (364 cal)

smoked salmon and mascarpone crepe cake

PREPARATION TIME 30 MINUTES (PLUS STANDING AND REFRIGERATION TIME) **COOKING TIME** 30 MINUTES

To make it easier to turn crepes, we used a heavy-base shallow non-stick frying pan.

¾ cup (110g) plain flour
3 eggs
1 tablespoon vegetable oil
1⅓ cups (330ml) milk
2 cups (500g) mascarpone
2 tablespoons prepared horseradish
2 tablespoons drained capers, rinsed, chopped coarsely
2 tablespoons finely chopped fresh tarragon
1 tablespoon finely grated lemon rind
500g sliced smoked salmon

MIXED PEA SALAD
300g sugar snap peas, trimmed
200g snow peas, trimmed
150g snow pea tendrils
2 tablespoons olive oil
2 tablespoons lemon juice

TIPS If the mascarpone is too soft, the crepe cake's refrigeration time may need to be increased. Crepes can be made up to two days ahead; wrap in plastic wrap and refrigerate until required. Crepe cake can be assembled the day before; store, covered, in refrigerator.

1 Line base and side of deep 22cm-round cake pan with plastic wrap.
2 Place flour in medium bowl. Make well in centre; gradually whisk in combined eggs, oil and milk. Strain batter into large jug, cover; stand 30 minutes.
3 Heat oiled 22cm non-stick frying pan; pour about ¼ cup of the batter into pan, tilting pan so batter coats base evenly. Cook crepe, over low heat, loosening around edge with spatula until browned lightly. Turn crepe; brown other side. Remove from pan; repeat with remaining batter to make a total of eight crepes.
4 Combine mascarpone, horseradish, capers, tarragon and rind in medium bowl; stir to combine. Place one crepe in prepared cake pan; spread with about ⅓ cup of the mascarpone mixture, cover with slices of salmon. Continue layering with remaining crepes, mascarpone mixture and salmon, finishing with crepe layer. Cover; refrigerate 3 hours or until firm.
5 Meanwhile, make mixed pea salad.
6 Cut crepe cake into eight wedges; serve with mixed pea salad.
   MIXED PEA SALAD Boil, steam or microwave sugar snap and snow peas, separately, until just tender; drain. Rinse under cold water; drain. Place sugar snap peas and snow peas in large bowl with remaining ingredients; toss gently to combine.

serves 8
per serving 50.3g fat; 2633kJ (629 cal)

curried blue-eye with lentils and raita

PREPARATION TIME 30 MINUTES **COOKING TIME** 45 MINUTES

1 cup (200g) brown lentils
1 cup (200g) green split peas
1 tablespoon vegetable oil
2 medium brown onions (300g), chopped finely
2 cloves garlic, crushed
4 dried curry leaves
2 bay leaves
2 cinnamon sticks
6 cardamom pods
6 cloves
½ teaspoon curry powder
¼ teaspoon ground coriander
1½ cups (375ml) chicken stock
4 x 200g blue-eye fillets, skinned
2 tablespoons mild curry paste
½ cup finely chopped fresh flat-leaf parsley

RAITA
2 lebanese cucumbers (260g), seeded
1 cup (280g) greek-style yogurt
1 tablespoon finely shredded fresh mint

1 Cook lentils and split peas in separate medium saucepans of boiling water, uncovered, until just tender; drain.
2 Meanwhile, make raita.
3 Heat oil in large frying pan; cook onion and garlic, stirring, until onion softens. Add leaves, cinnamon, cardamom, cloves, curry powder and coriander; cook, stirring, until fragrant. Add stock; cook, stirring, 2 minutes. Remove from heat.
4 Spread fish with curry paste; cook on heated oiled grill plate (or grill or barbecue) until browned both sides and cooked as desired.
5 Meanwhile, place lentils, split peas and parsley in frying pan with spicy onion mixture; stir over heat until heated through. Serve fish on lentil mixture; top with raita.
RAITA Grate cucumber coarsely; drain in fine sieve 10 minutes. Combine drained cucumber in small bowl with yogurt and mint.

serves 4
per serving 20.4g fat; 2869kJ (685 cal)

salt-baked whole ocean trout in saffron cream sauce

PREPARATION TIME 30 MINUTES **COOKING TIME** 1 HOUR 10 MINUTES

Cooking salt is coarser than table salt but not as large-grained as sea salt; it is sold packaged in bags, in most supermarkets. You need a large (approximately 28cm x 38cm) baking dish in order to accommodate the fish used in this recipe.

3kg cooking salt
4 egg whites
2.4kg whole ocean trout
1.5kg tiny new potatoes
3 whole unpeeled bulbs garlic, halved horizontally
¼ cup (60ml) olive oil
15 sprigs fresh thyme
350g watercress, trimmed

SAFFRON CREAM SAUCE
¾ cup (180ml) dry white wine
¼ cup (60ml) white wine vinegar
1 tablespoon lemon juice
pinch saffron threads
½ cup (125ml) cream
170g butter, chilled, chopped finely

1 Preheat oven to moderately hot.
2 Mix salt with egg whites in medium bowl (mixture will have the consistency of wet sand). Spread about half of the salt mixture evenly over the base of a large baking dish; place fish on salt mixture then cover completely (except for tail) with remaining salt mixture. Bake fish in moderately hot oven 1 hour.
3 Meanwhile, combine potatoes, garlic, oil and thyme in large shallow baking dish; place in oven on shelf below fish. Bake, uncovered, in moderately hot oven about 50 minutes or until potatoes are tender.
4 Make saffron cream sauce.
5 Remove fish from oven; break salt crust with heavy knife, taking care not to cut into fish. Discard salt crust; transfer fish to large serving plate. Carefully remove skin from fish; flake meat into large pieces.
6 Divide watercress, potatoes and garlic among serving plates; top with fish, drizzle sauce over fish.
SAFFRON CREAM SAUCE Combine wine, vinegar, juice and saffron in medium saucepan; bring to a boil. Boil until mixture is reduced to about a third. Add cream; return to boil, then whisk in butter, one piece at a time, until mixture thickens slightly. Pour into medium jug; cover to keep warm.

serves 6
per serving 50.7g fat; 3445kJ (823 cal)

bug and fennel risotto

PREPARATION TIME 30 MINUTES **COOKING TIME** 1 HOUR

Use either uncooked balmain bugs or moreton bay bugs for this recipe or, if you cannot find them, substitute fresh scampi.

2kg uncooked bugs
1 large fennel (550g)
¼ teaspoon black peppercorns
1 large brown onion (200g), quartered
1 trimmed celery stick (75g), chopped coarsely
1.625 litres (6½ cups) water
1½ cups (375ml) fish stock
40g butter
2 tablespoons olive oil
2 cloves garlic, crushed
2 cups (400g) arborio rice
1 cup (250ml) dry white wine
2 tablespoons coarsely chopped fresh chervil

1 Remove heads from bugs; discard contents, wash and reserve head shells. Cut through tails lengthways. Discard back vein from tail; remove and reserve bug meat.
2 Remove and reserve fennel stalks and green tips; halve and slice fennel bulb thinly, reserve.
3 Place head shells, fennel stalks and green tips, peppercorns, onion and celery in large saucepan with the water and fish stock; bring to a boil. Reduce heat; simmer, uncovered, 10 minutes. Strain stock into large heatproof bowl; discard solids. Return stock to same saucepan; bring to a boil. Reduce heat; simmer, covered.
4 Heat half of the butter with oil in large heavy-base saucepan; cook garlic and reserved fennel, stirring, until fennel softens. Add rice; stir to coat rice in butter mixture. Add wine; stir until wine reduces by half. Stir in 1 cup simmering stock; cook, stirring, over low heat until liquid is absorbed. Continue adding stock, in 1-cup batches, stirring until liquid is absorbed after each addition. Total cooking time should be about 35 minutes or until rice is just tender.
5 Add remaining butter and reserved bug meat to risotto; stir gently to combine. Stir in chervil just before serving.

serves 4
per serving 19.4g fat; 2961kJ (707 cal)

saganaki prawn ravioli

PREPARATION TIME 50 MINUTES **COOKING TIME** 20 MINUTES

Saganaki is the name given to any traditional Greek dish that combines baked or fried fetta with a tomato sauce.

¼ cup (60ml) extra virgin olive oil
5 large tomatoes (1.2kg), seeded, chopped coarsely
4 cloves garlic, crushed
¼ cup finely chopped fresh lemon thyme
700g uncooked medium prawns
⅓ cup (80g) sour cream
1 teaspoon finely grated lemon rind
200g fetta, crumbled
40 wonton wrappers

1 Heat 2 tablespoons of the oil in large saucepan; cook tomato, garlic and 2 tablespoons of the thyme, stirring, 2 minutes. Cover; cook over low heat for 5 minutes.

2 Meanwhile, shell and devein prawns; chop prawn meat coarsely. Combine prawn meat in medium bowl with sour cream, rind, 150g of the cheese and remaining thyme.

3 Centre a level tablespoon of the prawn mixture on one wrapper; brush around edges with water. Top with another wrapper, press edges together to seal. Repeat with remaining wrappers and filling; you will have 20 ravioli.

4 Cook ravioli, in two batches, in large saucepan of boiling water, uncovered, until ravioli float to the surface and are cooked through. Drain; divide ravioli among serving plates, top with hot tomato mixture, sprinkle with remaining cheese then drizzle with remaining oil. Top with extra thyme, if desired.

serves 4
per serving 35g fat; 2261kJ (540 cal)

macadamia prawn cakes

PREPARATION TIME 30 MINUTES **COOKING TIME** 30 MINUTES

¾ cup (180ml) orange juice
¼ cup (60ml) lemon juice
2cm piece fresh ginger (10g), chopped coarsely
1 teaspoon black peppercorns
2 tablespoons white vinegar
½ cup (125ml) dry white wine
½ cup (75g) toasted macadamias
750g cooked peeled small prawns
1 egg, beaten lightly
1 tablespoon finely grated orange rind
4 green onions, chopped finely
1½ cups (110g) stale breadcrumbs
1 long loaf pide
2 tablespoons vegetable oil
4 egg yolks
250g butter, melted
80g watercress

1 Combine juices, ginger, peppercorns, vinegar and wine in small saucepan; bring to a boil. Reduce heat; simmer, uncovered, about 8 minutes or until citrus mixture reduces to ½ cup. Remove from heat; strain into small jug.

2 Meanwhile, blend or process nuts until finely chopped; place in large bowl. Blend or process 500g of the prawns until mixture forms a paste; place in bowl with nuts. Add remaining prawns, egg, rind, onion and 1 cup of the breadcrumbs; using hands, shape mixture into eight cakes. Press remaining breadcrumbs on to both sides of cakes; place on tray.

3 Cut bread into four pieces; split each piece in half horizontally. Toast, cut-side up, under hot grill until browned lightly; cover to keep warm.

4 Heat oil in large frying pan; cook cakes, in batches, until browned both sides and heated through. Cover to keep warm.

5 Meanwhile, blend or process egg yolks with citrus reduction until combined. With motor operating, add butter in thin, steady stream; process until sauce thickens.

6 Place two pieces of toast on each serving plate; top with watercress then two cakes and drizzle with sauce.

serves 4
per serving 80.9g fat; 4943kJ (1181 cal)

tempura prawn salad

PREPARATION TIME 25 MINUTES   **COOKING TIME** 20 MINUTES

2cm piece fresh ginger (10g), chopped coarsely
¼ cup (60ml) soy sauce
¼ cup (60ml) mirin
2 tablespoons grated palm sugar
3 lebanese cucumbers (390g)
1 tablespoon drained sliced pink pickled ginger
1 small red onion (100g), halved, sliced thinly
100g mizuna
1 egg, beaten lightly
½ cup (75g) cornflour
½ cup (75g) plain flour
¾ cup (180ml) iced soda water
32 uncooked medium king prawns (1.5kg)
vegetable oil, for deep-frying

1   Press fresh ginger through garlic crusher into screw-top jar; add sauce,
     mirin and sugar, shake dressing until sugar dissolves.
2   Using vegetable peeler, slice cucumbers lengthways into thin strips. Cut
     pickled ginger slices into thin strips. Place cucumber and pickled ginger in
     large bowl with onion and mizuna; toss gently to combine.
3   Combine egg, flours and soda water in medium bowl, mixing lightly until just
     combined. Do not overmix, mixture should be lumpy. Stand 5 minutes.
4   Meanwhile, shell and devein prawns, leaving tails intact. Heat oil in wok or
     large saucepan; dip prawns in batter, one at a time, draining away excess.
     Deep-fry prawns, in batches, until browned lightly; drain on absorbent paper.
5   Pour half of the dressing over salad; toss gently to combine. Divide salad
     among serving plates; top with prawns, drizzle with remaining dressing.

serves 4
per serving 18.5g fat; 2243kJ (536 cal)

scallop mousse ravioli in star anise broth

PREPARATION TIME 40 MINUTES **COOKING TIME** 20 MINUTES

80g dried egg noodles
300g scallops, roe removed
2 tablespoons coarsely chopped fresh coriander
2 teaspoons finely chopped fresh lemon grass
1cm piece fresh ginger (5g), grated coarsely
2 tablespoons fish sauce
2 egg whites
1 litre (4 cups) chicken stock
1½ cups (375ml) fish stock
2 star anise
40 wonton wrappers
1 green onion
1 tablespoon drained sliced pink pickled ginger
1 fresh red thai chilli, seeded, sliced finely
⅓ cup firmly packed coriander leaves

1 Cook noodles in medium saucepan of boiling water until just tender; drain. Using kitchen scissors, chop noodles into random lengths; reserve.
2 Blend or process scallops, chopped coriander, lemon grass, fresh ginger, sauce and egg whites until mixture forms a smooth paste.
3 Bring stocks and star anise to a boil in large saucepan. Reduce heat; simmer, covered, while making ravioli.
4 Centre a level tablespoon of the scallop mixture on one wrapper; brush around edges with water. Top with another wrapper; press edges together to seal. Repeat with remaining wrappers and filling; you will have 20 ravioli.
5 Trim onion; cut crossways into quarters, cut each quarter lengthways into thin strips. Cut pickled ginger slices into thin strips. Divide onion, pickled ginger, noodles, chilli and coriander leaves among soup bowls.
6 Cook ravioli, in two batches, in same cleaned medium saucepan of boiling water, uncovered, until ravioli float to the surface and are cooked through. Drain; divide among bowls. Discard star anise from hot stock; ladle over ravioli.

serves 4
per serving 2.6g fat; 1107kJ (264 cal)

deep-fried perch with chilli lime dressing

PREPARATION TIME 15 MINUTES **COOKING TIME** 20 MINUTES

3 lebanese cucumbers (390g)
3 medium carrots (360g)
4 x 400g whole ocean perch, cleaned
vegetable oil, for deep-frying
½ cup (75g) plain flour
2 teaspoons salt
2 teaspoons ground white pepper

CHILLI LIME DRESSING

⅓ cup (80ml) sweet chilli sauce
2 teaspoons fish sauce
¼ cup (60ml) lime juice
1 teaspoon sesame oil
2 tablespoons coarsely chopped fresh thai basil
2 tablespoons coarsely chopped fresh vietnamese mint
2 tablespoons water

1 Using vegetable peeler, slice cucumbers and carrots lengthways into thin strips; combine in medium bowl.
2 Discard fish heads; score each fish three times both sides. Make chilli lime dressing.
3 Heat vegetable oil in wok or large saucepan. Combine flour, salt and pepper in medium shallow bowl; coat fish in flour mixture. Deep-fry fish, in two batches, until browned lightly and cooked through; drain on absorbent paper.
4 Divide carrot mixture among plates; top with fish, drizzle with dressing.
CHILLI LIME DRESSING Place ingredients in screw-top jar; shake well.

serves 4
per serving 16.2g fat; 1690kJ (404 cal)

sesame-seeded john dory fillets with kumara chips

PREPARATION TIME 30 MINUTES **COOKING TIME** 20 MINUTES

4 x 240g john dory fillets, skinned
½ cup (75g) sesame seeds
¼ cup (35g) plain flour
¼ cup (60ml) vegetable oil
vegetable oil, extra, for deep-frying
1 large kumara (500g), cut into 5mm slices
1 lime, cut into wedges

BEER BATTER
1 cup (150g) plain flour
1 teaspoon sweet paprika
1¼ cups (310ml) beer

1 Make beer batter.
2 Cut each fish fillet into three pieces. Combine seeds and flour in shallow medium bowl; coat fish in mixture.
3 Heat oil in large deep frying pan; cook fish, in batches, until browned both sides and cooked through. Cover to keep warm.
4 Meanwhile, heat extra oil in wok or large frying pan. Dip kumara slices in batter, draining away excess. Deep-fry kumara, in batches, until crisp and tender; drain on absorbent paper. Serve kumara topped with fish and lime wedges.
   BEER BATTER Whisk ingredients in medium bowl until smooth.

serves 4
per serving 40.9g fat; 3422kJ (818 cal)

singapore chilli crab

PREPARATION TIME 45 MINUTES (PLUS STANDING TIME) **COOKING TIME** 35 MINUTES

2 whole uncooked mud crabs (1.5kg)
2 tablespoons peanut oil
1 fresh long red chilli, chopped finely
2 cloves garlic, crushed
2cm piece fresh ginger (10g), grated
⅓ cup (80ml) chinese cooking wine
400g can crushed tomatoes
1 cup (250ml) water
1 tablespoon brown sugar
2 lebanese cucumbers (260g), halved lengthways, sliced thinly
10cm piece fresh ginger (50g), sliced thinly
3 green onions, sliced thinly
¼ cup loosely packed fresh coriander leaves
2 fresh long red chillies, seeded, sliced thinly

1 Place crabs in large container filled with ice and water; stand about 1 hour. Prepare crabs, leaving flesh in claws and legs (see page 110). Using cleaver or heavy knife, chop each body into sixths.

2 Heat oil in wok or large frying pan; stir-fry chopped chilli, garlic and grated ginger until fragrant. Add wine; cook until liquid has reduced by half. Add undrained tomatoes, the water and sugar; bring to a boil. Reserve half of the sauce in small bowl.

3 Add half of the crab to wok, reduce heat; simmer, covered, about 15 minutes or until crab has changed in colour. Stir in half of the cucumber. Transfer to large serving bowl; cover to keep warm. Repeat with reserved sauce, remaining crab and cucumber.

4 Cut sliced ginger into thin strips. Combine with onion, coriander and sliced chilli; sprinkle over crab. Serve with steamed jasmine rice, if desired.

serves 4
per serving 10.9g fat; 1103kJ (264 cal)

TIP Provide finger bowls filled with warm water and lemon slices – and plenty of large napkins – with this dish.

hot seafood platter

PREPARATION TIME 40 MINUTES (PLUS REFRIGERATION TIME) **COOKING TIME** 25 MINUTES

500g dhufish cutlets, skinned
500g calamari rings
1 cup (150g) plain flour
¼ cup (60ml) milk
4 eggs, beaten lightly
2 cups (140g) stale breadcrumbs
⅓ cup finely chopped fresh flat-leaf parsley
½ cup (40g) finely grated parmesan cheese
1 tablespoon finely grated lemon rind
1 medium tomato (190g), halved
1 tablespoon vodka
¼ teaspoon Tabasco sauce
2 teaspoons worcestershire sauce
1 teaspoon lemon juice
vegetable oil, for shallow-frying
12 oysters, on the half shell
1 trimmed celery stick (75g), chopped finely
3 slices pancetta (45g), chopped finely
8 uncooked large king prawns (560g)
2 lemons, cut into wedges

1 Halve fish lengthways, discard bones; cut each half into three pieces. Coat fish and calamari in flour, then in combined milk and egg, and finally in combined breadcrumbs, parsley, cheese and rind. Cover; refrigerate 15 minutes.
2 Meanwhile, using largest holes on a four-sided grater, grate tomato halves, from cut-side, into small bowl; discard skin. Stir in vodka, sauces and juice.
3 Heat oil in large deep frying pan; shallow-fry fish and calamari, in batches, until browned and cooked through. Drain on absorbent paper.
4 Meanwhile, place oysters on oven tray. Divide tomato mixture among oysters; top with celery and pancetta. Place under hot grill about 5 minutes or until pancetta is crisp.
5 Cook prawns on heated oiled grill plate (or grill or barbecue) until browned lightly and cooked through. Arrange seafood and lemon wedges on large serving platter.

serves 4
per serving 58.4g fat; 4572kJ (1092 cal)

TIP You can substitute your favourite white fish fillets for the dhufish in this recipe.
SERVING SUGGESTION Serve with dipping sauces from the cold seafood platter (page 96).

cold seafood platter with dipping sauces

PREPARATION TIME 1 HOUR

1 cooked large lobster (1.2kg)
2 cooked blue swimmer crabs (650g)
4 cooked balmain bugs (800g)
16 cooked large king prawns (1.1kg)
12 oysters, on the half shell
3 lemons, cut into wedges

1 Prepare lobster (see page 110). Pat dry with absorbent paper.
2 Prepare crabs (see page 110). Rinse well under cold water; cut crab bodies into halves.
3 Place bugs upside-down on chopping board; cut in half lengthways. Remove any green matter, liver and back vein from tails.
4 Shell and devein prawns, leaving heads and tails intact.
5 Arrange seafood on large serving platter with lemon. Serve with dipping sauces.

serves 4
per serving (without dipping sauces) 4.2g fat; 1706kJ (407 cal)

DIPPING SAUCES

sambal mayonnaise

PREPARATION TIME 5 MINUTES

½ cup (150g) mayonnaise
1 tablespoon water
2 tablespoons tomato sauce
1 teaspoon worcestershire sauce
1 teaspoon sambal oelek

Combine ingredients in small bowl.

makes ¾ cup
per tablespoon 5.4g fat; 281kJ (67 cal)

soy and mirin

PREPARATION TIME 5 MINUTES

2 tablespoons water
1 tablespoon soy sauce
2 tablespoons mirin
2 teaspoons rice vinegar
½ teaspoon sambal oelek

Combine ingredients in small bowl.

makes ½ cup
per tablespoon 0g fat; 43kJ (10 cal)

mustard and dill

PREPARATION TIME 5 MINUTES

½ cup (150g) mayonnaise
1 tablespoon water
1 tablespoon drained baby capers, rinsed
1 teaspoon wholegrain mustard
1 tablespoon coarsely chopped fresh dill

Combine ingredients in small bowl.

makes ⅔ cup
per tablespoon 6.1g fat; 296kJ (71 cal)

chilli and lime

PREPARATION TIME 5 MINUTES

¼ cup (60ml) sweet chilli sauce
2 tablespoons lime juice
1 tablespoon water
1 teaspoon fish sauce
2 teaspoons finely chopped fresh vietnamese mint

Combine ingredients in small bowl.

makes ½ cup
per tablespoon 0.3g fat; 56kJ (13 cal)

trevally mornay pies

PREPARATION TIME 25 MINUTES **COOKING TIME** 35 MINUTES

2½ cups (625ml) milk
½ small brown onion (40g)
1 bay leaf
6 black peppercorns
4 x 170g trevally fillets, skinned
3 large potatoes (900g), chopped coarsely
600g celeriac, chopped coarsely
1 egg yolk
½ cup (40g) finely grated parmesan cheese
¾ cup (180ml) cream
60g butter
¼ cup (35g) plain flour
2 tablespoons coarsely chopped fresh flat-leaf parsley

1 Place milk, onion, bay leaf and peppercorns in large saucepan; bring
   to a boil. Add fish, reduce heat; simmer, covered, about 5 minutes
   or until cooked through. Remove fish from pan; divide fish among
   four 1½-cup (375ml) ovenproof dishes. Strain milk through sieve into
   medium jug. Discard solids; reserve milk.
2 Boil, steam or microwave potato and celeriac, separately, until tender;
   drain. Push potato and celeriac through sieve into large bowl; stir in
   yolk, cheese, ¼ cup of the cream and half of the butter until smooth.
   Cover to keep warm.
3 Meanwhile, melt remaining butter in medium saucepan; add flour,
   cook, stirring, about 3 minutes or until mixture bubbles and thickens
   slightly. Gradually stir in reserved milk and remaining cream; cook,
   stirring, until mixture boils and thickens. Stir in parsley.
4 Divide mornay mixture among dishes; cover each with potato mixture.
   Place pies on oven tray; place under hot grill until browned lightly.

serves 4
per serving 47.7g fat; 3478kJ (831 cal)

seafood risoni paella

PREPARATION TIME 30 MINUTES **COOKING TIME** 30 MINUTES

Paella is traditionally made by Spaniards using short-grain white
rice but, for an interesting alternative, try risoni, a tiny short pasta
that adds a smoother texture to the finished dish.

12 uncooked medium king prawns (540g)
250g small mussels
300g piece ling
2 tablespoons olive oil
1 small brown onion (80g), chopped finely
4 cloves garlic, crushed
500g risoni
pinch saffron threads
1 cup (250ml) dry white wine
6 small tomatoes (780g), seeded, chopped coarsely
2 tablespoons tomato paste
1 teaspoon finely grated orange rind
4 sprigs fresh marjoram
1 litre (4 cups) vegetable stock, warmed
1½ cups (185g) frozen peas
150g calamari rings

1 Shell and devein prawns, leaving tails intact. Scrub mussels;
   remove beards. Cut ling into 3cm pieces.
2 Heat oil in large deep frying pan; cook onion and garlic, stirring,
   until onion softens. Add risoni and saffron; stir to coat in onion
   mixture. Stir in wine, tomato, paste, rind and marjoram; cook,
   stirring, until wine has almost evaporated.
3 Add 1 cup of the stock, stirring, until absorbed. Add remaining
   stock; cook, stirring, until risoni is almost tender.
4 Place peas and seafood in pan on top of risoni mixture; do not stir
   to combine. Cover pan, reduce heat; simmer about 10 minutes
   or until seafood has changed in colour and mussels have opened
   (discard any that do not).

serves 4
per serving 14.3g fat; 3352kJ (801 cal)

TIP This recipe can be made in a traditional paella pan if you own
one; otherwise a deep frying pan or wok having a tight-fitting lid will
suffice. Serve the paella straight from the pan at the table.

malaysian swordfish curry

PREPARATION TIME 25 MINUTES **COOKING TIME** 35 MINUTES

Shallots, also called french shallots, golden shallots or eschalots, are small, elongated members of the onion family that grow in tight clusters, similarly to garlic. You will need approximately 2 sticks fresh lemon grass for this recipe.

6 fresh red thai chillies, chopped coarsely
2 cloves garlic, quartered
10 shallots (120g), chopped coarsely
½ cup coarsely chopped fresh lemon grass
5cm piece galangal (25g), quartered
1 teaspoon curry powder
1 teaspoon ground coriander
¼ teaspoon ground turmeric
2 tablespoons vegetable oil
1 tablespoon fish sauce
1⅔ cups (400ml) coconut milk
1⅔ cups (400ml) coconut cream
2 cups (400g) jasmine rice
4 x 220g swordfish steaks, skinned
¼ cup (10g) flaked coconut, toasted
4 kaffir lime leaves, shredded finely

1   Blend or process chilli, garlic, shallot, lemon grass, galangal, curry powder, coriander, turmeric and half of the oil until mixture forms a paste.
2   Heat remaining oil in large frying pan; cook paste, stirring, over medium heat about 3 minutes or until fragrant. Add sauce, coconut milk and cream; bring to a boil. Reduce heat; simmer, uncovered, about 15 minutes or until mixture thickens slightly.
3   Meanwhile, cook rice in large saucepan of boiling water, uncovered, until tender; drain. Cover to keep warm.
4   Cook swordfish on heated oiled grill plate (or grill or barbecue), in batches, until browned both sides and cooked as desired.
5   Divide fish among serving bowls; top with sauce, sprinkle with toasted coconut and lime leaves. Serve rice in separate bowl.

serves 4
per serving 59.5g fat; 4667kJ (1115 cal)

TIP   If you can't find shallots, substitute a medium brown onion and a small clove of crushed garlic.

blackened ocean trout fillets with burnt-butter risotto

PREPARATION TIME 25 MINUTES **COOKING TIME** 45 MINUTES

1 teaspoon sweet paprika
1 tablespoon dried thyme
1 tablespoon dried oregano
1 teaspoon cayenne pepper
2 teaspoons garlic powder
4 x 220g ocean trout fillets, with skin

BURNT-BUTTER RISOTTO

2 cups (500ml) water
2 cups (500ml) vegetable stock
80g butter
1 tablespoon olive oil
1 cup (250ml) dry white wine
1 medium brown onion (150g), chopped finely
1 clove garlic, crushed
1¼ cups (250g) arborio rice
¼ cup finely chopped fresh flat-leaf parsley
¼ cup (20g) finely grated parmesan cheese

1 Combine spices, herbs and garlic powder in medium bowl; using fingers, press spice mixture into skin-side of fish fillets. Cover fish; refrigerate.

2 Meanwhile, make burnt-butter risotto.

3 Cook fish in large lightly oiled non-stick frying pan, skin-side up, until browned lightly. Turn; cook fish until skin browns and fish is cooked as desired. Serve fish, skin-side up, on risotto.

BURNT-BUTTER RISOTTO Combine the water and stock in medium saucepan; bring to a boil. Reduce heat; simmer, covered. Heat butter and oil in large saucepan until butter begins to brown slightly. Add wine; cook until liquid reduces by half. Add onion and garlic; cook, stirring, until onion softens. Add rice; stir to coat in onion mixture. Stir in ½ cup of the simmering stock; cook, stirring, over low heat, until liquid is absorbed. Continue adding stock, in ½-cup batches, stirring, until liquid is absorbed between each addition. Total cooking time should be about 35 minutes or until rice is tender. Stir in parsley and cheese.

serves 4
per serving 33g fat; 3205kJ (766 cal)

south-east asian salmon parcels with fresh mango sauce

PREPARATION TIME 30 MINUTES   **COOKING TIME** 15 MINUTES

½ small leek (100g)
⅓ cup loosely packed fresh coriander leaves
1 large red capsicum (350g), sliced thinly
1 teaspoon five-spice powder
½ teaspoon ground coriander
1 tablespoon grated palm sugar
1 tablespoon lime juice
4 x 220g salmon fillets, skinned
4 x 21.5cm-square spring roll wrappers
1 tablespoon cornflour
2 teaspoons water
⅓ cup (80ml) peanut oil
2 medium mangoes (860g), chopped coarsely
100g red coral lettuce

1 Cut leek into 8cm lengths; halve each piece lengthways then slice halves into thin strips. Combine leek in small bowl with fresh coriander and half of the capsicum.

2 Preheat oven to moderately hot.

3 Heat small lightly oiled frying pan; cook five-spice and ground coriander, stirring, until fragrant. Stir in sugar and juice; remove from heat. When cool enough to handle, use fingers to rub half of the spice mixture into both sides of salmon fillets.

4 Place a salmon fillet on bottom half of one spring roll wrapper; top with a quarter of the leek mixture. Lightly brush edges of wrapper with blended cornflour and water; roll to enclose salmon, folding in ends. Repeat with remaining salmon, wrappers, leek mixture and cornflour mixture.

5 Heat oil in large frying pan; cook parcels, in batches, until browned lightly. Place on oiled oven tray; bake parcels in moderately hot oven about 8 minutes or until fish is cooked as desired.

6 Meanwhile, blend or process half of the mango and remaining spice mixture until smooth. Combine remaining mango, remaining capsicum and lettuce in large bowl. Serve salmon parcels with salad topped with mango sauce.

serves 4
per serving 35.4g fat; 2677kJ (639 cal)

TIPS Brown sugar can be substituted for palm sugar.
Parcels can be made up to 30 minutes ahead; refrigerate, covered with a slightly dampened tea towel.

how to prepare seafood

follow our easy step-by-step techniques

butterflying small fish

Discard the head then slice lengthways down along entire underside of each fish; remove and discard entrails.

Use your thumb (or a small rolling pin) to press down along entire length of backbone to ensure the fish lies flat.

Carefully work a sharp heavy knife under the backbone to lift it, pulling it out without tearing the flesh.

preparing shellfish

Cooked or raw, the head of a shellfish is removed by holding it in one hand then twisting the body with the other.

Peel away the legs and shell from the shellfish body, but leave the tail intact, if you like, for decorative purposes.

Remove and discard the centre vein from the back of each shellfish, using a small sharp knife or your fingers.

preparing crab

Cooked or raw, crab is shelled the same way: lift tail flap then, with a peeling motion, lift off the back shell.

Remove and discard the whitish gills (known as dead men's fingers), liver and brain matter; rinse crab well.

Crack body shell and remove the meat, then crack claw shells carefully to avoid getting splinters of shell amid the flesh.

preparing lobster

With the lobster upside-down, cut through the chest and tail; turn lobster around and cut through the head.

Pull halves apart; use a small spoon to remove brain matter and liver. Rinse lobster carefully under cold water.

Remove lobster meat from the shell with your fingers; it should lift out easily in a single large piece.

preparing balmain bugs

Balmain and moreton bay bugs are usually sold already cooked. Turn bug upside-down before cutting off head.

Cut bug tail in half lengthways using a sharp knife; carefully lift out and remove the centre vein from tail.

Use the fingers of one hand to pull out from the shell the entire chunk of bug flesh, keeping it intact if possible.

shucking oysters

Wrap a tea towel around each oyster as you lever a knife into the hinge, twisting it until the shells pop apart.

Loosen oyster from shell with the tip of a small sharp knife; try to reserve the oyster liquor for added natural flavour.

preparing mussels

Clean the uncooked fresh mussels thoroughly by scrubbing them well all over with a stiff kitchen brush.

Pulling the "beard" down and away from the mussel's hinge makes removing it much faster and easier.

preparing squid

  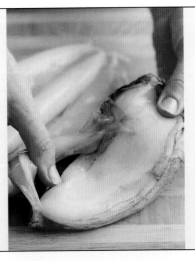

Gently pull head and entrails away from the squid body, then remove the clear quill (backbone) and discard it.

Cut tentacles from head just below eyes of squid; remove the beak in the same way that you do on an octopus.

Pull away the purple-tinged membrane from the squid hood and flaps (wings); wash hood, tentacles and flaps well.

preparing octopus

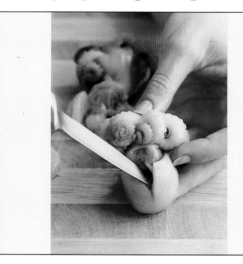  

Slit down the back of the octopus head using a small sharp knife then use your fingers to pull out the entrails.

Make a small cut deep into the centre of the tentacles; pop the beak out through the hole and then discard it.

Cut out the eyes and discard them; wash tentacles and head thoroughly under cold running water.

preparing sashimi

Before slicing fish for carpaccio or sashimi, wrap it tightly in plastic wrap then freeze it until it is just firm.

Using a heavy sharp knife, slice the just-frozen fish as thinly as possible as soon as it is removed from the freezer.

fish varieties

NAME AND VARIETIES	DESCRIPTION AND COOKING TECHNIQUES
Blue-eye (trevalla): also known as bigeye, blue-eye trevalla, deepsea trevalla, ocean blue-eye, sea trevally. Substitute with snapper, kingfish.	Delicate flavour and moist flaky flesh. Firm texture. Flesh is off-white in colour. Sold mostly in fillets and cutlets. Suited to all methods of cookery.
Bream (yellowfin): also known as silver bream, seabream, surf bream, black bream. Substitute with snapper, ocean perch.	Soft, white, delicate flesh. Moist with a mild flavour. Sold whole and in fillets. Bake, pan-fry, barbecue, poach, grill.
Flake: also known as school shark, snapper shark, tope. Substitute with ling.	Boneless white flesh with a distinct but subtle flavour; this is the most popular species used in fish and chip shops. Sold as skinless fillets. Deep-fry, pan-fry, barbecue, stir-fry.
Gemfish: also known as southern kingfish, hake, silver kingfish, king couta.	Mild-flavoured fish having a moist firm texture. Available as fillets and smoked. Pan-fry, bake, barbecue, grill, poach.
Jewfish: also known as mulloway. Substitute with blue-eye, kingfish.	Firm white flesh with a mild flavour. Grill, barbecue, bake, pan-fry, poach, steam. Do not overcook as flesh will become quite dry.
John dory: also known as st peter's fish, kuparu. Substitute with blue-eye, bream.	Firm fine texture. Sweet, moist, white flesh. Expensive. Steam, barbecue, grill, poach, deep-fry, bake, pan-fry.
Kingfish (yellowtail): also known as southern yellowfish, kingie, tasmanian yellowtail. Substitute with jewfish.	Full flavour and firm slightly dry flesh. Excellent fish for sashimi and smoking. Sold whole, in fillets or in cutlets. Eat raw, barbecue, bake, grill, pan-fry, smoke.
Leatherjacket: also known as file fish, ocean jacket, cream fish, silver flounder.	Mild-flavoured white flesh. Soft moist texture. Skin should always be removed before consuming. Sold whole (with head removed) or as fillets. Bake, grill, pan-fry, steam.
Ling: available in two varieties, rock and pink. Substitute with flake, hake.	Long eel-like body. Firm texture, white flesh. Moist, mild and delicate in flavour. Pink variety can grow up to 20kg in weight. Bake, grill, steam, barbecue, poach, pan-fry, stir-fry.
Mahi mahi: also known as dolphin fish, dorado. Substitute with swordfish, mako shark, striped marlin.	Firm texture and mild flavour. Sold in steaks or fillets without skin. Grill, barbecue, bake, poach, pan-fry. Can also be used in curries or stews.
Ocean perch: also known as coral perch, coral cod, sea perch, red perch. Substitute with snapper.	Delicate flavour. Firm white flesh. Steam, poach, pan-fry, grill.
Ocean trout. Substitute with salmon.	Orange/pink oily flesh. Firm but delicate moist texture; sweet flavour. Sold fresh or smoked, whole, in fillets or in cutlets. Barbecue, grill, poach, steam, pan-fry.
Red emperor. Substitute with snapper, goldband snapper.	Firm and flaky texture with a delicate moist flavour. Mostly sold without skin. Barbecue, grill, bake, steam, pan-fry, deep-fry.
Salmon: also known as atlantic salmon. Substitute with ocean trout, blue-eye.	Oily fish with orange/pink flesh. High in omega-3 fats. Rich distinctive flavour. Sold fresh or smoked, whole, in fillets or in cutlets. Eat raw, smoke, cure, steam, poach, bake, barbecue, grill, pan-fry.
Sardines: also known as pilchards. Substitute with garfish.	Soft oily flesh. Small species up to 18cm long; strong but pleasant flavour. Buy whole or as butterflied fillets. High in omega-3 fats. Shallow-fry, bake, grill, barbecue, smoke.
Smoked cod. Substitute with smoked haddock.	Smoky flavour, firm flesh. Sold whole or as fillets. Pan-fry, grill, steam, bake.
Snapper: also known as pink snapper, red bream, squire, cockney. Substitute with bream, sea perch, red emperor.	Delicate flavour and succulent flesh; a versatile and popular fish suited to all methods of cookery.

NAME AND VARIETIES	DESCRIPTION AND COOKING TECHNIQUES
Swordfish: also known as broadbill. Substitute with yellowfin tuna, bluefin tuna, mahi mahi.	Flesh is pale pink in colour and has a fine firm texture. Sold in steaks or cutlets. Grill, bake, pan-fry; can also be cooked in curries and soups. Do not overcook.
Trevally (silver trevally): also known as skippy, jack. Substitute with warehou.	Firm, pink, slightly oily flesh; mild to strong flavour. Eat raw (depending on flesh quality), barbecue, grill, casserole, bake, pan-fry, poach.
Tuna: available in many varieties including yellowfin, longtail, bluefin, skipjack, albacore. Substitute with swordfish.	Dark-red, oily flesh with firm/dense texture. A very popular fish to eat raw. Sold whole or in cutlets, steaks or fillets. Shallow-fry, bake, grill, smoke.
Whiting (sand whiting): also known as silver whiting, summer whiting, king george whiting, trumpeter. Substitute with bream.	Fine-textured white flesh having a sweet delicate flavour. Available whole or in fillets. Bake, barbecue, grill, pan-fry, poach.

crustaceans & molluscs

NAME AND VARIETIES	DESCRIPTION AND COOKING TECHNIQUES
Baby octopus. Substitute with octopus, squid.	Firm texture with a sweet mild flavour. Marinating before cooking helps tenderise the flesh. Grill, pan-fry, steam, stir-fry, smoke. Do not overcook.
Balmain bug: also known as slipper or shovelnose lobster, southern bay lobster. Substitute with moreton bay bugs, king prawns, scampi.	Distinctive sweet flavour; moist texture. Pan-fry, barbecue, grill, bake, steam.
Blue swimmer crab: also known as blue crab, blue manna crab, bluey, sand crab, sandy. Substitute with lobster, balmain bugs, moreton bay bugs.	Soft sweet flesh. Sold whole or as crab meat. Steam, poach, bake, stir-fry, grill, barbecue.
King prawn: also known as ocean king, blueleg, sand, western, western king. Substitute with scampi, farmed tiger prawns.	Sweet true-prawn flavour; moist firm flesh. Buy uncooked or cooked. Look for good colour and lustre, and shells free of discolouration. Steam, poach, deep-fry, shallow-fry, stir-fry, barbecue, grill. Becomes tough if overcooked.
Lobster (rock lobster): also known as crayfish, cray, spiny lobster, eastern, southern or western lobster. Substitute with balmain bugs, moreton bay bugs.	Eastern rock lobsters are green in colour when uncooked — western and southern are both red/orange when uncooked. Flesh has a firm texture and sweet rich flavour. Poach, steam, barbecue, grill, pan-fry.
Moreton bay bug: also known as flat head lobster, gulf or bay lobster, mudbug. Substitute with balmain bugs, king prawns, scampi.	Sweet flavour; firm moist texture. Pan-fry, barbecue, grill, bake, steam.
Mud crab: also known as green crab, black crab, mangrove crab. Substitute with scampi, lobster, balmain bugs.	An estuary species, has a dark-green/brown shell. Buy live or cooked. Moist, flaky, sweet flesh. Steam, poach, bake, stir-fry, grill, barbecue.
Mussel. Varieties include: black, green-lip.	Both varieties have a moist texture and distinct "sea flavour". Eat raw, bake, barbecue, grill, pan-fry, steam. Flesh becomes tough if overcooked.
Oyster: available in many varieties including pacific oyster, bay/blacklip oyster, sydney/new zealand rock oyster.	Flavour varies among varieties, but each has a moist soft texture. Eat raw, grill, bake, deep-fry.
Pipi: also known as beach pipi, eugarie, clam, coorong cockle. Substitute with surf clam, cockle, vongole.	Sweet but slightly chewy flesh. Can be eaten raw. Barbecue, poach, stir-fry, steam. Great in chowders and pasta sauces.
Scallop: available in two main varieties, tasmanian (also known as southern or king scallop) and queensland (also known as saucer or mud scallop).	Both varieties are moist in texture. Tasmanian has creamy white flesh with orange/red roe. Queensland has paler flesh that is slightly sweeter and firmer than the tasmanian. Grill, barbecue, steam, poach, pan-fry, stir-fry.

We should like to thank the Sydney Fish Market for its invaluable help in the compilation of this book.

glossary

ALLSPICE also known as pimento or Jamaican pepper; so-named because it tastes like a combination of nutmeg, cumin, clove and cinnamon. Is available whole (a pea-sized dark-brown berry) or ground, and used in both sweet and savoury dishes.

BACON RASHERS also known as slices of bacon, made from pork side, cured and smoked.

BOK CHOY also called pak choi or chinese white cabbage; has a fresh, mild mustard taste and is good braised or in stir-fries. Baby bok choy is also available and is slightly more tender than bok choy.

BROCCOLINI a cross between broccoli and chinese kale; milder and sweeter than broccoli. Each long stem is topped by a loose floret that closely resembles broccoli; from floret to stem, broccolini is completely edible.

BUTTER use salted or unsalted ("sweet") butter; 125g is equal to one stick of butter.

CAPSICUM also known as bell pepper or, simply, pepper. Native to Central and South America, capsicums come in many colours: red, green, yellow, orange and purplish-black. Be sure to discard seeds and membranes before use.

CARDAMOM native to India and used extensively in its cuisine, this spice can be purchased in pod, seed or ground form.

CAYENNE PEPPER a long, extremely hot red chilli usually sold dried and ground.

CELERIAC tuberous root with brown skin, white flesh and a celery-like flavour.

CHERVIL also known as cicily; herb with mild fennel flavour and curly leaves.

CHICKPEAS also called garbanzos, channa or hummus; round, sandy-coloured legumes.

CHILLIES generally the smaller the chilli, the hotter it is. Use rubber gloves when seeding and chopping fresh chillies to avoid burning your skin.
ancho (called poblano chillies when fresh) fruity, sweet, and quite smoky in flavour, they measure about 8cm in length and are dark reddish-brown in colour.
flakes, dried deep-red, dehydrated chilli slices and whole seeds; good for use in cooking or as a condiment for sprinkling over cooked foods.
thai red also known as "scuds"; small, very hot and bright red. Can be substituted with fresh serrano or habanero chillies.

CLOVES dried flower buds of a tropical tree; can be used whole or in ground form. Have a distinctively pungent and "spicy" scent and flavour.

COCONUT
cream available in cans and cartons; made from coconut and water.
desiccated unsweetened, concentrated, dried, finely shredded coconut.
milk not the juice found inside the fruit, but the diluted liquid pressed from the white meat of a mature coconut. After the liquid settles, the cream and "milk" (thin white fluid) separate naturally. Available in cans or cartons.

CORIANDER also known as cilantro or chinese parsley; bright-green leafy herb with a pungent flavour. Also sold as seeds, whole or ground.

CORNFLOUR also known as cornstarch; used as a thickening agent in all types of cooking.

CORNICHONS from the French word for "gherkin", these are minuscule pickled gherkins used to accompany pâtés or as a condiment with salads.

COUSCOUS a fine, grain-like cereal product, originally from North Africa; made from semolina.

CURRY POWDER a blend of ground spices used for convenience when making Indian food. Can consist of some of the following spices in varying proportions: dried chilli, cinnamon, coriander, cumin, fennel, fenugreek, mace, cardamom and turmeric. Choose mild or hot to suit your taste and the recipe.

DAIKON also known as giant white radish. Used extensively in Japanese cooking; has a sweet, fresh flavour without the bite of the common red radish. Can be used raw in salads and as a garnish, or cooked in various ways.

EGG some recipes call for raw or barely cooked eggs; exercise caution if there's a salmonella problem in your area.

EGGPLANT purple-skinned vegetable also known as aubergine. Can also be purchased char-grilled, packed in oil, in jars.

FISH SAUCE also called nam pla or nuoc nam; made from pulverised salted fermented fish, most often anchovies. Has a pungent smell and strong taste; use sparingly.

FIVE-SPICE POWDER fragrant ground mixture of cinnamon, cloves, star anise, sichuan pepper and fennel seeds.

FLAT-LEAF PARSLEY also known as continental parsley or italian parsley.

FLOUR, PLAIN an all-purpose flour, made from wheat.

GAI LARN also known as gai lum, chinese broccoli or chinese kale, this vegetable is prized more for its stems than its coarse leaves. Can be eaten stir-fried on its own or tossed into various soups and noodle dishes.

GALANGAL a rhizome with a hot ginger-citrusy flavour; used similarly to ginger and garlic. Substitute with fresh ginger if unavailable.

GARAM MASALA a blend of spices based on varying proportions of cardamom, cinnamon, cloves, coriander, fennel and cumin, roasted and ground together.

GINGER also known as green or root ginger; the thick root of a tropical plant. Pickled ginger is sold in pieces or sliced, and comes in red and pink varieties packed in a seasoned brine.

HORSERADISH CREAM a commercially prepared creamy paste made of grated horseradish, vinegar, oil and sugar.

KAFFIR LIME LEAVES aromatic leaves of a citrus tree; used similarly to bay leaves, usually in Thai cooking.

KECAP MANIS also known as ketjap manis; a thick soy sauce with added sugar and spices.

KITCHEN STRING made of a natural product such as cotton or hemp so that it neither affects the flavour of the food it is tied around nor melts when heated.

KUMARA Polynesian name of orange-fleshed sweet potato, often confused with yam.

LAKSA PASTE a bottled paste containing lemon grass, chillies, galangal, shrimp paste, onions and turmeric.

LEBANESE CUCUMBER short, thin-skinned and slender; also known as the european or burpless cucumber.

MINCE also known as ground meat.

MIRIN sweet rice wine used in Japanese cooking; not to be confused with sake.

MUSHROOMS
porcini also known as cèpes; aromatic and earthy-flavoured, available both fresh and dried; the latter are reconstituted and used in many classic Italian dishes such as risottos and pasta sauces.
shiitake when fresh are also known as chinese black, forest or golden oak mushrooms; although cultivated, have the earthiness and taste of wild mushrooms. When dried, known as donko or dried chinese mushrooms; rehydrate before use.

MUSTARD
seeds, black also known as brown mustard seeds; more pungent than the yellow (or white) seeds.
wholegrain also known as seeded mustard; a coarse-grain mustard made from black and yellow mustard seeds and dijon-style mustard.

NOODLES
bean thread also known as bean thread vermicelli, cellophane noodles or glass noodles.
rice soft white noodles made from rice flour and vegetable oil; available in varying thicknesses, from vermicelli-thin to broad and flat. Rinse under hot water to remove starch and excess oil before usi

PALM SUGAR also known as jaggery, jawa or gula melaka; made from the sap of the sugar palm tree. Light brown to black in colour and usually sold in rock-hard cakes; substitute it with brown sugar if unavailable.

PANCETTA cured pork belly; substitute with bacon.

PIDE also known as turkish bread. Comes in long (about 45cm) flat loaves as well as individual rounds; made from wheat flour and sprinkled with sesame or black onion seeds.

PINK PEPPERCORNS dried berries usually sold packed in brine (occasionally found freeze-dried); have a distinctive pungently sweet taste that goes well with fish and cream sauces.

POLENTA also known as cornmeal; a flour-like cereal made of dried corn (maize) sold ground in different textures; also the name of the dish made from it.

PRESERVED LEMON a North African speciality, the citrus is preserved in a mixture of salt and lemon juice. Can be rinsed and eaten as is, or added to casseroles and tagines for a rich salty-sour flavour.

PROSCIUTTO cured, air-dried, pressed ham; usually sold thinly sliced.

REDCURRANT JELLY a preserve made from redcurrants; used as a glaze for desserts and meats, or in sauces.

SAKE rice wine used in cooking or as a drink. If unavailable, substitute dry sherry or brandy.

SAMBAL OELEK (also ULEK or OLEK) Indonesian in origin; a salty paste made from ground chillies.

SCAMPI similar to a prawn but much larger.

SEAFOOD some recipes in this book call for raw or uncooked fish and other seafood; exercise caution if there's a salmonella problem in your area.

SHALLOTS also called french shallots, golden shallots or eschalots; small, brown-skinned, elongated members of the onion family that grow in tight clusters similarly to garlic.

SHRIMP PASTE also known as trasi or blanchan; a strong-scented, almost solid preserved paste made of salted dried shrimp. Used as a pungent flavouring in many South-East Asian soups and sauces.

SPRING ONION vegetable having a small, white, walnut-sized bulb, long green leaves and narrow green-leafed tops.

STAR ANISE a dried star-shaped fruit of a tree native to China. The pods, which have an astringent aniseed or licorice flavour, are widely used in the Asian kitchen. Available whole or ground.

TAMARI a thick, dark soy sauce made mainly from soy beans without the wheat used in standard soy sauce.

TAMARIND CONCENTRATE the commercial distillation of tamarind pulp into a condensed paste. Use straight from the container, with no soaking or straining required; dilute with water according to taste.

THAI BASIL has smallish leaves and sweet licorice/aniseed taste; it is one of the basic flavours that typify Thai cuisine. Available in Asian supermarkets and greengrocers.

TOMATO SAUCE also known as ketchup or catsup; a condiment made from tomatoes, vinegar and spices.

VIETNAMESE MINT a narrow-leafed, pungent herb; also known as cambodian mint or laksa leaf.

ZUCCHINI also known as courgette; small green, yellow or white vegetable belonging to the squash family.

make your own stock

These recipes can be made up to 4 days ahead and kept, covered, in the refrigerator. Remove any fat from the surface after the cooled stock has been refrigerated overnight. If stock is to be kept longer, freeze it, divided into smaller quantities. All the recipes below make approximately 2.5 litres (10 cups) of stock.

Stock is also available in cans or cartons; stock cubes or powder can also be used. As a guide, 1 teaspoon of stock powder or 1 small crumbled stock cube mixed with 1 cup (250ml) water will result in a fairly strong stock. Be aware of the salt and fat content of these products.

chicken stock

2kg chicken bones
2 medium onions (300g), chopped
2 sticks celery, chopped
2 medium carrots (250g), chopped
3 bay leaves
2 teaspoons black peppercorns
5 litres (20 cups) water

Combine ingredients in large pan, simmer, uncovered, 2 hours; strain.

fish stock

1.5kg fish bones
3 litres (12 cups) water
1 medium onion (150g), chopped
2 sticks celery, chopped
2 bay leaves
1 teaspoon black peppercorns

Combine ingredients in large pan, simmer, uncovered, 20 minutes; strain.

index

facts + figures

Wherever you live, you'll be able to use our recipes with the help of these easy-to-follow conversions. While these conversions are approximate only, the difference between an exact and the approximate conversion of various liquid and dry measures is minimal and will not affect cooking results.

dry measures

metric	imperial
15g	1/2oz
30g	1oz
60g	2oz
90g	3oz
125g	4oz (1/4lb)
155g	5oz
185g	6oz
220g	7oz
250g	8oz (1/2lb)
280g	9oz
315g	10oz
345g	11oz
375g	12oz (3/4lb)
410g	13oz
440g	14oz
470g	15oz
500g	16oz (1lb)
750g	24oz (11/2lb)
1kg	32oz (2lb)

oven temperatures

These oven temperatures are only a guide. Always check the manufacturer's manual.

	°C (Celsius)	°F (Fahrenheit)	Gas Mark
Very slow	120	250	1
Slow	150	300	2
Moderately slow	160	325	3
Moderate	180 – 190	350 – 375	4
Moderately hot	200 – 210	400 – 425	5
Hot	220 – 230	450 – 475	6
Very hot	240 – 250	500 – 525	7

liquid measures

metric	imperial
30ml	1 fluid oz
60ml	2 fluid oz
100ml	3 fluid oz
125ml	4 fluid oz
150ml	5 fluid oz (1/4 pint/1 gill)
190ml	6 fluid oz
250ml	8 fluid oz
300ml	10 fluid oz (1/2 pint)
500ml	16 fluid oz
600ml	20 fluid oz (1 pint)
1000ml (1 litre)	13/4 pints

helpful measures

metric	imperial
3mm	1/8in
6mm	1/4in
1cm	1/2in
2cm	3/4in
2.5cm	1in
5cm	2in
6cm	21/2in
8cm	3in
10cm	4in
13cm	5in
15cm	6in
18cm	7in
20cm	8in
23cm	9in
25cm	10in
28cm	11in
30cm	12in (1ft)

measuring equipment

The difference between one country's measuring cups and another's is, at most, within a 2 or 3 teaspoon variance. (For the record, 1 Australian metric measuring cup holds approximately 250ml.) The most accurate way of measuring dry ingredients is to weigh them. When measuring liquids, use a clear glass or plastic jug with the metric markings. (One Australian metric tablespoon holds 20ml; one Australian metric teaspoon holds 5ml.)

If you would like to purchase *The Australian Women's Weekly* Test Kitchen's metric measuring cups and spoons (as approved by Standards Australia), turn to page 120 for details and order coupon. You will receive:

- a graduated set of four cups for measuring dry ingredients, with sizes marked on the cups.
- a graduated set of four spoons for measuring dry and liquid ingredients, with amounts marked on the spoons.

Note: North America, NZ and the UK use 15ml tablespoons. All cup and spoon measurements are level.

We use large eggs having an average weight of 60g.

how to measure

When using graduated metric measuring cups, shake dry ingredients loosely into the appropriate cup. Do not tap the cup on a bench or tightly pack the ingredients unless directed to do so. Level top of measuring cups and measuring spoons with a knife. When measuring liquids, place a clear glass or plastic jug with metric markings on a flat surface to check accuracy at eye level.

Looking after **your interest...**

Keep your ACP cookbooks clean, tidy and within easy reach with slipcovers designed to hold up to 12 books. Plus you can follow our recipes perfectly with a set of accurate measuring cups and spoons, as used by *The Australian Women's Weekly* Test Kitchen.

To order

Mail or fax Photocopy and complete the coupon below and post to ACP Books Reader Offer, ACP Publishing, GPO Box 4967, Sydney NSW 2001, or fax to (02) 9267 4967.

Phone Have your credit card details ready, then phone 136 116 (Mon-Fri, 8.00am-6.00pm; Sat, 8.00am-6.00pm).

Price

Book Holder

Australia: $13.10 (incl. GST).
Elsewhere: $A21.95.

Metric Measuring Set

Australia: $6.50 (incl. GST).
New Zealand: $A8.00.
Elsewhere: $A9.95.

Prices include postage and handling. This offer is available in all countries.

Payment

Australian residents

We accept the credit cards listed on the coupon, money orders and cheques.

Overseas residents

We accept the credit cards listed on the coupon, drafts in $A drawn on an Australian bank, and also British, New Zealand and U.S. cheques in the currency of the country of issue. Credit card charges are at the exchange rate current at the time of payment.

Photocopy and complete coupon below

- -

☐ **Book Holder**

☐ **Metric Measuring Set**
Please indicate number(s) required.

Mr/Mrs/Ms _____

Address _____

_____

Postcode _____ Country _____

Ph: Business hours ( ) _____

I enclose my cheque/money order for $ _____ payable to ACP Publishing.

OR: please charge my

☐ Bankcard ☐ Visa ☐ Mastercard

☐ Diners Club ☐ American Express

| | | | | | | | | | | | | | | | |

Card number

Expiry date ____ /____

Cardholder's signature _____

Please allow up to 30 days delivery within Australia. Allow up to 6 weeks for overseas deliveries. Both offers expire 31/12/04. HLDS03

Test Kitchen Staff
Food director *Pamela Clark*
Food editor *Karen Hammial*
Assistant food editor *Amira Ibram*
Test Kitchen manager *Kimberley Coverdale*
Senior home economist *Cathie Lonnie*
Home economists *Belinda Black, Sammie Coryton, Kelly Cruickshanks, Christina Martignago, Jessica Sly, Kate Tait, Alison Webb*
Editorial coordinator *Rebecca Steyns*

ACP Books Staff
Editorial director *Susan Tomnay*
Creative director *Hieu Chi Nguyen*
Senior editor *Lynda Wilton*
Designer *Anna Lazar*
Studio manager *Caryl Wiggins*
Editorial/sales coordinator *Caroline Lowry*
Editorial assistant *Karen Lai*
Publishing manager (sales) *Brian Cearnes*
Publishing manager (rights & new projects) *Jane Hazell*
Brand manager *Donna Gianniotis*
Pre-press *Harry Palmer*
Production manager *Carol Currie*
Business manager *Sally Lees*
Assistant business analyst *Martin Howes*
Chief executive officer *John Alexander*
Group publisher *Jill Baker*
Publisher *Sue Wannan*

Produced by ACP Books, Sydney.
Printed by Dai Nippon Printing in Korea.
Published by ACP Publishing Pty Limited, 54 Park St, Sydney; GPO Box 4088, Sydney, NSW 2001.
Ph: (02) 9282 8618 Fax: (02) 9267 9438.
acpbooks@acp.com.au
www.acpbooks.com.au
To order books, phone 136 116.
Send recipe enquiries to: recipeenquiries@acp.com.au
AUSTRALIA: Distributed by Network Services, GPO Box 4088, Sydney, NSW 2001.
Ph: (02) 9282 8777 Fax: (02) 9264 3278.
UNITED KINGDOM: Distributed by Australian Consolidated Press (UK), Moulton Park Business Centre, Red House Rd, Moulton Park, Northampton, NN3 6AQ.
Ph: (01604) 497 531 Fax: (01604) 497 533
acpukltd@aol.com
CANADA: Distributed by Whitecap Books Ltd, 351 Lynn Ave, North Vancouver, BC, V7J 2C4.
Ph: (604) 980 9852 Fax: (604) 980 8197
customerservice@whitecap.ca
www.whitecap.ca
NEW ZEALAND: Distributed by Netlink Distribution Company, ACP Media Centre, Cnr Fanshawe and Beaumont Streets, Westhaven, Auckland.
PO Box 47906, Ponsonby, Auckland, NZ.
Ph: (9) 366 9966 ask@ndcnz.co.nz

Clark, Pamela.
The Australian Women's Weekly
Dinner seafood.

Includes index.
ISBN 1 86396 314 6.
1. Cookery (Seafood). I. Title.
II. Title: Australian Women's Weekly.
641.692

© ACP Publishing Pty Limited 2003
ABN 18 053 273 546

First published 2003.

The publishers would like to thank the following for props used in photography:
Accoutrement, Mosman, NSW
Country Road HomeWear
Design Mode International, Mona Vale, NSW
Mud Australia, Marrickville, NSW
Village Living, Avalon, NSW
Villeroy & Boch
Wheel & Barrow